D0593395

Praise for
THE LEADER'S CLIMB

"This is a wonderful story that offers important insights into rising to the challenge of leadership today."
—Marshall Goldsmith, million-selling author of
New York Times best-sellers *MOJO* and *What Got You Here Won't Get You There*

"The recommended-reading list for a business leader is extensive, with new books from well-known authors, such as Jim Collins (*Great by Choice,* 2011, and others), and ones by new writers, such as journalist Charles Duhigg's *The Power of Habit* (2012). Yet business leaders should pay attention here, because executive coaches Parsanko and Heagen have captured an important business trend, the art of listening, which has been noticed by the *McKinsey Quarterly.* Although that particular lesson isn't necessarily the one they espouse—instead, they point to going too fast, fighting too much, and forcing too many decisions—it is the heart of fictional CEO protagonist Adam and his almost-fall from glory, literally and figuratively. During his vacation, Adam has a rock-climbing accident, and while recovering, he meets contractor Duncan and trail-guide A. J., who provide teachable moments in the midst of his disagreement with the board of directors about a possible acquisition. Good things to learn here, especially considering that 85 percent of today's CEOs are new 'top dogs' and are expected to remain only about 3.5 years in their positions."   —*Booklist*

"This is a powerful, evocative, and realistic tale of good leaders trying to climb the next mountain. If more people took this story to heart, they would be better leaders."

—Ted Nixon, Former International Executive Chair, Young Presidents' Organization (YPO) and CEO, DD Williamson, Inc.

"People are not born great leaders. They develop skills over a lifetime that come together into a leadership approach. *The Leader's Climb* rings with truth, depth, and realism, and will challenge you to grow continually as a leader."

—Matthew Kelly, *New York Times* best-selling author of *The Dream Manager*

"Wow! This may be a tale, but it sure feels amazingly real. The message in this book is powerful and timely."

—Mike Monahan, author of Inc. #1 best-seller *From the Jungle to the Boardroom*

"*The Leader's Climb* is a cause for self-reflection and discovery. It is an engaging story that has applications both personally and professionally for those who connect with its message."

—Susan Croushore, CEO, The Christ Hospital, Cincinnati

"This book couldn't be more timely or relevant to the challenges leaders are facing. Through an artful story, it makes a powerful case for slowing down to avoid being a casualty of today's break-neck pace of business. I wish all executives would take the time to read this—it is that different and that important."

—Jim Anderson, former Director, Executive Education, Kelley Graduate School of Business, Indiana University

"Adam's story is repeated every day by well-intentioned business leaders trying to get a grip on the never-ending struggles we all face. While the signs of decline may not be obvious, they are insidious. The three key messages in this book identify these signs and the remedies in ways that are personally and professionally meaningful."

—Larry Grypp, President, Goering Center for Family and Private Business, Lindner College of Business, University of Cincinnati

"This book is an easy read covering three important and often overlooked elements of leadership. For more than 20 years Bob Parsanko has helped us build a successful global organizational culture based on these principles and guided our key executives, including me, to become better leaders."

—Mogens Bay, Chairman and CEO, Valmont Industries, Inc.

"*The Leader's Climb* carries an elegant, useable message for all leaders who care to be the best they can be while creating great and enduring organizations."

—Al Stuempel, Master Chair, Vistage International, Inc.

The

LEADER'S
CLIMB

The
LEADER'S
CLIMB

A Business Tale

OF RISING TO THE NEW

LEADERSHIP CHALLENGE

BOB PARSANKO

PAUL HEAGEN

Anderson County Library
Anderson, S.C.

bibliomotion
books + media

First published by Bibliomotion, Inc.
33 Manchester Road
Brookline, MA 02446
Tel: 617-934-2427
www.bibliomotion.com

Copyright ©2012 by Bob Parsanko and Paul Heagen.

All rights reserved. No part of this publication may be reproduced in any manner whatsoever without written permission from the publisher, except in the case of brief quotations embodied in critical articles or reviews.

Printed in the United States of America
ISBN 978-1-937134-21-1

Library of Congress Cataloging-in-Publication Data

Parsanko, Bob.
    The leader's climb : a business tale of rising to the new leadership challenge / Bob Parsanko and Paul Heagen.
        p.   cm.
    ISBN 978-1-937134-21-1 (hardcover : alk. paper)—
ISBN 978-1-937134-22-8 (ebook)—
ISBN 978-1-937134-23-5 (enhanced ebook)
    1. Leadership.   I. Heagen, Paul.   II. Title.
    HD57.7.P3656 2012
    658.4'092—dc23

                                                    2012027874

Foreword

Today in companies big and small, local and global, public and private, leaders at all levels say the same thing: business has become faster, more complicated, more uncertain, more disruptive and more competitive. There is nowhere to hide. The forces of technology, information, transparency, globalization, and customer choice wash over everything. We all feel the force and the pressure.

To be a leader today one must constantly improve if only to survive, much less gain ground. It is natural that we search for every edge—new ideas, different systems, better processes, and clearer procedures in the hopes of getting more and more done faster and faster. We believe that if only we can get ahead of the deluge we can get control, make sense of it all, and then, finally, have time to think and plan.

Unfortunately, this does not happen.

Going faster, becoming more efficient, making longer lists—using one's "head" to solve it once and for all will not work. It takes heart and guts, as well. There is too much to "figure out" and so one must be able to use multiple senses, including intuition, experience, analogies, and stories. A leader today must learn to integrate multiple and subtle data and feelings. To lead in an increasingly complex world today means becoming a whole leader—and regrettably there is no manual with checklists for doing so.

But there is this book, *The Leader's Climb.* It's not another set of lists, but rather a story: a realistic, thoughtful, and provocative story that requires us to slow down, become absorbed, feel it as much as read it, and allow oneself to have an experience. In that experience—call it a space of intentional quiet—as we read about another leader, we are called to connect with our own sense of self, our purpose, our personal source of leadership resolve and identity. That is the magic of this book.

The Leader's Climb is the story of Adam, but it is also the story of the Adam in each of us. Hurried, trying to do too much, confident, unconscious—we know him because we have all lived parts of his life. Adam's predicament, which we all share, is that he cannot see his own blind spots, and yet he plunges blindly ahead anyway. Fortunately, he meets some very capable coaches and teachers on his path whose wisdom and compassion create some new awareness and behaviors. As the story progresses Adam learns that coaches are everywhere, as is the opportunity each of us has to grow through acceptance and understanding.

Many companies today are led by those who resemble Adam in this story. It's not hard to see the impact on organizations of leadership that focuses primarily on speed, efficiency, results, and financial return. The same issues come up over and over again. The tyranny of the urgent becomes a substitute for planning and prioritization. Snap decisions with hidden costs replace careful consideration with obvious time requirements. Mindless compliance replaces community and commitment. Activity that looks like momentum disguises chaos. Purpose is sacrificed to performance at any cost. And sadly, as senior management teams go, so go their companies.

It is a small wonder there are so many business books published to deal with this issue. But the last thing we need is another quick read with a task list at the end of each chapter. The real problem is we don't need more to *do*. We need to know the right things to do, which is usually gained through deeper awareness of ourselves, others, and the context in which we are leading.

The message in *The Leader's Climb* is simple, but it becomes clear to the reader why it is so hard to carry it out. In these pages you will see how failure is hardly ever a singular, cataclysmic event, but more often a slow but steady erosion of self and a sense of purpose that can eventually consume even the most talented and earnest leaders. You will learn, as Adam does, that "form" can never replace "substance," and that to be a true leader means being true to one's inner voice, not the outer demands and expectations, which will never be tamed or satisfied. My hope is that you will come to appreciate Adam's leadership struggles as they unfold, his awareness develops, and some important principles of leadership are uncovered.

Almost from the beginning of time man has learned from great stories. Timeless truths have been passed from generation to generation through teaching tales, which indirectly show us what is right as well as real. Stories help us learn with our heart, as well as our head. In *The Leader's Climb*, we have a modern version of the classic Hero's Journey. In this retelling, Adam's journey is through the external obstacles of modern business life. But the real Hero's Journey, as Adam discovers, is inward. In this simple allegory, authors Parsanko and Heagen help us understand the inner path to self-awareness and better leadership, and they offer us confidence that we can each get there.

We live in a noisy world of information and stimulus overload. Our attention is fragmented. We rush, we hurry, and we do more, faster and faster. And then something happens that jars us awake and makes us realize we don't need to do more, we need to listen more. We need quiet space, and the discipline and ability to command time and spend it reflecting, learning, listening and ultimately making decisions when it is time to make them, not just to dispense with them so we can move on to the next one. For me, this book created such a space. And I hope it does for you.

David L Dotlich
Chairman, Pivot Leadership
author of *Why CEOs Fail*, and *Head, Heart and Guts*

Part I

STUCK

One

———

Adam was stuck.

The work to this point had been almost easy, familiar—and largely without obstacles. Three years into his first job as CEO, his place in life felt natural. He was just drawing on what had made him a success all along— talent and drive, a dash of charm, but more than anything, confidence.

Confidence, as Adam saw it, laid bare your opportunities, put your skills to the test, and muffled that inner voice that sometimes rose up too early and too often, injecting self-doubt. Most obstacles are not new, they are just different enough to throw you off. Certainly, something in your experience can serve you, no matter your situation; it is just a matter of knowing how to apply it.

Yet, he had to admit, this time he was stuck.

I can't stay in this predicament, he scolded himself. I don't do *stuck*.

Adam pressed himself tighter against the dark tan surface to recenter his gravity so he could look below and to the side without falling. His right foot was angled into a crevice in the rock but his left foot relied on friction alone to stay planted on the smooth wall of the boulder.

He was far from worried, and panic was another world away. One foot wedged, another sucking the side of the boulder, fingertips curled white-knuckled into shallow recesses, he was plenty safe. Still, he had to admit, he was not going anywhere the way things stood.

The boulder was a stretch for the more casual rock climber, jutting about fifteen feet up from a smooth granite slab. It was one of the larger boulders that Adam took on during his hikes through the canyon near his vacation home, but it was not the kind that had ever posed a problem before. Adam had free-climbed rocks like these back when he was in college, when he and his buddies would hike in for a couple of days to get away from the books, get a good burn going in their arms and legs, and just fill their lungs with some clear air.

Today, if this boulder had been any taller or tougher, he would not have taken it on. You save that bravado for when you are not alone. With the responsibilities he had back in Chicago, he could take risks, but not stupid gambles. Get it wrong and you are there with cramping muscles, aching toes and fingers, and a surface suddenly bereft of handholds or safe ledges. At times like that, an invisible gravity just hauls on you.

His plan had been to traverse the face of the boulder at a shallow angle, following the whisper of a seam that barely split the smooth surface. But now that he was up here living it, the next foothold and the next handhold were just out of reach. He could work his way back down, but Adam knew that stepping back posed its perils. Going down, oddly, put you more at the mercy of gravity.

The slight momentum of moving down was sometimes enough to overcome friction and send you flying.

Several minutes had passed while Adam patiently sized up his situation, but now it was time to make a move. Make something happen. Anything but *stuck*.

He reached down carefully with one hand to knead the chalk bag suspended on his belt, coating his fingers with powder, then did the same with the other hand. Steeled with a renewed resolve, he figured the next hand-hold option was not so unreasonable. He would just have to time everything right and make a catlike move to the next mooring, letting his momentum overcome the relentless pull of gravity. He wriggled his fingertips to lock in their grip on the bare dents in the wall above and mentally practiced his next move as if it were a ballet: slide his left foot up to the next coarse section to get some grip and then rock himself upward just enough to trust leaving the right foot's anchor spot and replaster his hands and feet on the next set of coordinates.

The process of realizing his situation and deliberating what to do about it took more time than he realized. Adam now was feeling the heat of the sun on his neck; sweat began to bead on his arms and trickle down his legs. Salty perspiration glistened on his eyelids and he shook his head quickly to fling the drops away so they did not distract him.

Move. Go.

He hoisted himself up ever so slightly so he could wrest his right foot from its foothold. His body seemed suddenly heavy as his fingers and left foot clung to the cliff, waiting for his right foot to find a place to share the load.

People always say accidents—the bad ones—seem to happen in slow motion. This time, the whole event compressed and seemed to happen all at once—he felt his arms quivering, heard a scraping sound, felt the scuff of the wall against his face, felt his fingers and toes slip out of their roosts, saw the blue sky and the burning sunlight filling up the frames of his sunglasses as he fell away from the wall.

Sorry, Maureen . . . Jason . . .

A white-hot jolt of pain rocketed up from his right heel and he heard a thick *crunch* as his helmet thumped heavily against the ground before all went dark.

"So, you think this is enough for us to get started?"

The man with the blue chambray shirt, khaki pants, and sandals looked up from the clipboard lying on the kitchen table when he heard Adam's question. "It's a start, yes."

Despite the throb of his headache, Adam still had to fight to suppress a smile as he gazed down at the paper. Other than the "Duncan Reynolds—Home Remodeling" neatly printed across the top, the page was little more than handwritten notes, a column of numbers, and a sketch.

"Then let's do it!" Adam said, as he punched the trigger on a ballpoint pen, then stroked his signature on the line at the bottom of the page and spun the clipboard back toward the other man. He hoisted himself up on his crutches, circling to face the double doors to the backyard.

"So, Mr. Reynolds, do we begin with the sunroom or should we do the whole backyard at the same time?"

"You can call me Duncan." The workman rolled the paper sketch into his weathered palm and joined Adam to gaze at the backyard. "As far as the whole project, it depends on what you want."

"Well, I'm ready to have us do it all as soon as we can." Adam was trying hard to keep the conversation at an easy pace, but his leg and head were in competition to see which one could throb the most. "For now, at least, how long on the sunroom?"

"For the sunroom..." Duncan unfurled the sketch as if to remind himself of what was involved, "I'm thinking three weeks, assuming we don't run into anything. I can start in about a month..."

"A month?" Adam whistled quietly then turned to face Duncan. "Can we move it up at all? I'm only here on vacation for two weeks and I need to be comfortable with how it's going. I am hosting my board of directors out here in September. I don't want to cut it close." Adam never liked to issue directives without lending a hand to carry them out if needed, and this was no different. "Hey, I can be out there with you every day to answer questions or address anything that comes up. Whatever it takes."

Duncan pointed down to Adam's bandage-wrapped foot and the crutches. "You ready to be out there every day like that?"

"Oh yeah. It's just a bad sprain. It's my head that hurts." Adam shrugged. "So, what do you say? Can we move this thing up?"

"Well," said Duncan, "it depends."

"On?" Adam looked up and fired off a beseeching smile.

Duncan folded the sketch and slipped it into a zippered notepad case, thumping the case on the table as if to gain time for his response.

"I'll have to let you know."

Adam leaned against the foam pads of his crutches and lightly punched the heel of his hand against the contractor's shoulder.

"Well, let me know soon. This can be a great project, you know…"

Duncan tucked the tablet under his arm and reached out to shake Adam's hand.

"That's what I want, too."

Two

———

It was the pounding in his head that woke Adam three mornings after the accident. The painkillers had rinsed away the throbbing in his leg but the misery just seemed to transport itself and beat his brains in with a thick thudding that matched each heartbeat.

The doctor said the concussion was nothing serious, so the headache would probably go away after a few days. You don't want to go cold turkey and flush the pills, he warned Adam. Trust me, he told him, it's going to hurt for a while. Don't fight it, he said.

Or you'll lose.

The disorientation—the feeling that he was a little off-balance—was only aggravated by the pain pills. The gnawing sense that he had to force a stride or a sense of rhythm to his day had been with him for several weeks, if not months. That's why he liked the idea of the vacation, as ill-timed as it may have been, with the acquisition just weeks away. Getting that deal put together internally had been far more difficult than Adam imagined, and it turned out to be real heavy lifting to get the board of directors lined up and staying put. So, getting in some rock climbing, some casual reading, and just mellowing out in the open air would recharge him, which was especially important before the final negotiations and the closing. He was never fully *away* from the buzz of activity at the office, but he accepted that. The cell phone and laptop were always there, especially with the deal being worked. Timing is everything, even if the timing intrudes into your personal life, a reality he and his wife, Maureen, had learned to accept as part of his CEO role.

The remodeling was all part of this trip—at least he could get it well underway, answer the questions, and make sure the plans were being executed, then Maureen could stay behind and make sure it got finished while Adam went back to Chicago. The investment bankers said a couple of weeks was fine, as long as he kept tabs on things and was there when they drafted the term sheets.

The pounding seemed to be getting worse. Lying in bed alone—Maureen was already up rattling plates in the kitchen—Adam realized the thudding no longer matched the rhythm of his pulse. Was he imagining it, or was it coming from outside?

Adam gingerly swung his legs to the side of the bed, reached for the crutches, and hoisted himself upright. He pawed across the carpet, balanced on his good leg, and speared the curtain with one of the crutches to pull it back from the window and peer outside to the backyard.

He couldn't see anything or anybody, but their border collie, Ollie, was pacing around on the patio, lowering his head and sniffing in the direction of the porch, just out of Adam's field of view. He wrapped a robe around himself and hobbled into the kitchen.

"They started," Maureen said, looking up from her magazine at the snack bar. "That was quick. You must have done your charm school thing on him."

"Hey, it worked on you years ago." Adam gritted through his headache to wink at Maureen and then wrenched the handle on the French doors. He swung the tips of his crutches out onto the patio, careful not to snag the rubber cups in the mortar cracks.

The backyard was the same as the day before—bare and empty—but to his left he saw a man hunched over near the base of one of the posts on the overhang that sheltered the steps running along the back of the house. A high school–age boy was next to the man, wearing work gloves and boots. The workman was wielding a heavy mallet, striking it firmly against the base of a post, which shuddered with each blow. After one last healthy swing, the wood splintered, prompting Adam to wince, his swollen leg dangling above the patio surface. The boy gathered up the broken post and dragged it to a gravel area near the driveway.

The workman rose from his crouch and turned to face Adam.

"Morning."

It was Duncan, all right, only now he was dressed in baggy carpenter overalls with a black shirt. He wore thick, weathered boots that were speckled with paint and drywall compound. A bright yellow tape measure dangled from a belt loop and his upper pocket bristled with a phalanx of broad, industrial-grade pencils. His rumpled painter's cap barely contained the mop of rusty red hair that curled loosely down the sides of a tanned and creased face that spoke to years in the sun, framed by a nearly trimmed but thick, mostly gray beard. Poking out of a side pocket, waving and bouncing lazily, was a cluster of thick, dark strands of some kind of braided material.

Duncan flipped back the cap, dropped the sledge to the ground, and wiped a rivulet of sweat from his forehead with the back of his hand. Adam leaned against the crutches in silence as Ollie warily paced an imaginary perimeter around the stranger.

"You made it—earlier than you thought," Adam said with a satisfied air.

"I had my reasons," Duncan said.

"Well, I'm hoping the reason is that we need to get this done!" Adam laughed appreciatively.

"I'm just glad it worked out for both of us." Duncan held out his open palm to Ollie, who eyed it warily then backed away. The boy, who looked to be about sixteen years old, came back around the side of the house. He was dressed in jeans and boots, but not the same beefy work clothes as Duncan. He busied himself in the background picking up scraps of wood and shingles, tossing them in a dumpster hooked to the back of Duncan's pale blue king cab pickup truck.

Adam returned his eyes to the scene around him. Fresh two-by-fours were jammed upright into the corners of the porch overhang and two of the regular posts were already on the ground, victims of hammer blows.

"So, where is the plan?" Adam spoke just loud enough to be heard; any louder, his head would start pounding again. "Do you have the project prints?"

"I have what I need for now, right up here," Duncan tapped an index finger against his temple. "A little early to lock in on any detailed plans…" He sucked in a deep breath and turned back toward the posts.

"Don't you use blueprints or something?" Adam clenched the handles of his crutches as the hammer blows renewed. Adam wasn't sure whether Duncan couldn't hear him over the *crack* of the mallet or was just not responding.

"Wait!" Adam skipped forward on his good leg and balanced himself against the wall. "Shouldn't we stop taking things apart until we have a plan?"

Duncan let the mallet slip out of his hardened hands and tumble to the ground with a muffled thud, and he pushed back his cap. "Are you planning to keep all these old posts and this porch overhang?"

"Well, no. Of course not," Adam said, puzzled.

"Okay, so all I'm doing is clearing them out, getting them out of the way." Duncan swept his hand across the expanse of the porch. "Hard to see where you want to go when your view is taken up by old stuff. Removing what does *not* matter is the first step in figuring out what *does*."

Adam scanned the growing stack of timbers, and then sagged a bit on his crutches, looking down at the patio to gather his thoughts.

"Trust me on this," Duncan said, letting his gaze linger on Adam for some sign that Adam was relaxing at all. Adam closed his eyes for a moment and nodded in cautious assent, but the drumming of his fingers against the handles of the crutches betrayed some lingering nervousness. Duncan's face crinkled into a grin as he retrieved the mallet and hoisted it over his head.

Adam watched him for several minutes. Duncan's moves were steady, practiced, and powerful. After a while, it was clear that the porch posts were not just randomly collapsing from reckless assaults by the hammer but were yielding to measured blows. One, two, three—*crack*. Each time. Each pillar. As the sledge shattered a pillar, Duncan muscled it with his shoulder to break out the last few splinters holding it in place, easing it to the ground so the boy could drag it away.

On one of the next posts, Duncan handed the mallet to the boy, adjusting the boy's grip on the handle. The teenager punched at the post with a sharp, short swing. Duncan stood next to him and swung his empty hands in a wide, steady arc, occasionally gripping the head of the mallet to guide the direction and pace of the boy's swing. Duncan nodded approval at one point and the boy turned back to the post to renew his work.

"Okay, once we get all this out of there, then do we go over the project plan?" Adam bit his lip, a little embarrassed that he was jumping back to his earlier plea.

Duncan waved to the boy to keep working and stood up to address Adam.

"We will, yes," Duncan said. "But there will be more for us to discuss before that. Right now, first things first. By the way," Duncan pointed to the youth, "this is Cole. He's my sidekick for a few days."

Adam smiled broadly and waved at the boy, then swung back toward the house, skipped across the threshold of the door, and lurched into the kitchen. He rested his crutches against the kitchen counter and slumped down in one of the chairs as Maureen looked up again from her morning reading.

"He and the kid are going at it, Mo," Adam murmured, attempting to keep his headache at bay. "I have to admit, I'm a little nervous that we don't have a plan yet. I just want this to be nice for you."

"I'm sure it will be fine," she said. "Anyway, you said you wanted to get the project started." Maureen flipped a page of the magazine and glanced down at the pages as she kept a nonchalant tone in her voice. "You had some more calls from Chicago while you were still in bed—Beth, Mort, Darrell. They sure are worried about you. I don't think they would like you up and about so soon."

"That was nice." Adam's closed his eyes. "I'll drop them a note as soon as I get a second."

Maureen studied his face for a moment. "I'm surprised. You don't look excited about that."

"No, it's not that." Adam punched his finger rapidly, nervously, against the granite counter. "It just makes me uncomfortable not having a plan for the backyard, not having things locked down. We need this to be done right." Adam flipped open his laptop on the kitchen counter, skimmed through his e-mails, then slapped the lid closed. He shuffled through the stack of mail on the counter, retreating to the den with an outdoor magazine and a catalog of sports gear. Maureen heard him ease onto the leather couch and flip on the TV. After a few minutes, she could hear his steady, deep breathing and the sound of the magazine tumbling to the floor.

An hour later, Adam ventured back out onto the patio, gripping a stainless steel travel mug of coffee in one hand and swinging one crutch by pinching it against the side of his chest with his forearm. He settled into a patio chair and watched as Duncan took out the last of the posts and Cole clumped the broken remains into a neat pile near the driveway. Adam finished his coffee and was letting the pain pills sink him more deeply into the lounge chair, when he was startled by the gentle *slap* of a paper tablet landing on the patio table.

"What's this?" Adam called out to Duncan, who was walking back toward the truck. The paper was largely blank, with a simple question written out in neat letters on the top line:

What do you want?

"Hey, Dunc," Adam called out, "what's that mean?"

"Just something to keep your mind active," Duncan said as he lifted fresh timbers from the back of the truck and stacked them against a wall.

"You mean for the backyard, right?" Adam said louder, to be heard over the sound of the lumber being slapped against the wall. Duncan nodded slightly and returned to work. Adam was never comfortable with questions that seemed to lack focus and purpose. They reminded him of the couple of semesters in college when he had played baseball. Give me a high fastball, Adam thought—I'll take it and send it over the fence. But those loopy changeups— crazy, no way to do anything with them.

Adam felt a little exasperated. "Geez, Dunc, that's why I was hoping you would share your project plans with me in the first place."

"We'll get to the project plans in due time," Duncan said with a wink, "but first, think about the question. Really. Let's take care of that first." Duncan walked back around the corner of the house to gather more timbers.

Adam then heard Duncan's deep voice echo from around the side of the house.

"And, it's Duncan," the voice said. "My name is Duncan."

⌒

Adam was not sure what time it was when he woke up, but the sun was hovering directly overhead. The backyard was quiet; Duncan and Cole were out of sight. Adam lifted himself out of the lounge chair, grabbed his crutches, and went into the kitchen.

"You and Duncan making some progress?" Maureen asked impishly.

"Hard to say," Adam sighed. "He's motoring right through the demolition work, that's for sure. All the more reason I wish we could nail down the details for the new sunroom."

Maureen speared flowers one by one into a vase. "Funny, because he told me this morning that he was going to have the two of you start talking about the whole plan. Are you sure you weren't dozing off?"

"You're so good to me, Mo..."

Maureen turned around from the sink and tossed a hand towel across the kitchen at Adam.

"I'm good *for* you, too, buster," she laughed.

Adam heard Ollie barking and looked outside to see Duncan coming around the corner from the driveway and crouching in front of the collie, reaching into his pocket for one of the braided strands Adam had seen earlier. Duncan waved it in front of Ollie, who sniffed it but then backed away and went back under the shade of the porch.

Ollie's fussy, Adam mouthed silently in Duncan's direction. He doesn't take kindly to strangers, and he doesn't fall easily for someone trying to make friends.

"Good luck with that," Adam laughed to himself, as he turned back toward the den.

Three

———

"I'm going up to the rock, Mo," Adam announced the next morning as he clomped past Maureen in the kitchen and headed out toward the backyard.

"You're not serious!"

"I'm going crazy in the house," he sighed. "Bad ankle or not, I'm not about to spend my vacation cooped up here. And I am afraid if I stick around here too much, Duncan will want to discuss his question."

"What question?" Maureen peered at Adam with a curious look.

"Something about what I want—for the project," Adam shrugged. "It's not that hard a question, so I'm not sure why I'm sitting here thinking about it so much. I guess I'm not sure what he needs.

"Anyway," he said, balancing himself to grasp the door handle, "I'm going to the rock."

Barely four days on crutches and he wants to go back to the scene of the crime, Maureen thought. She talked with the doctor at the hospital and he had said that Adam should give it a week. Even if the ankle felt better, the concussion needed some time. She plucked the cell phone from the counter and stuffed it in his pocket.

"I know better than to try to stop you, especially since you seem to be a little on edge lately. Here, take this with you," she said, giving him an affectionate slap on the shoulder. "Nine-one-one. You might want to put it on speed dial." She laughed as she opened the French doors for him and feigned booting him with the side of her foot.

That morning, Duncan and Cole had already cleared the sparse sod from underneath the deconstructed awning. Duncan was crouched down with a carpenter's bubble level, steering Cole's eyes down a line of yellow string suspended between two stakes. Duncan began knifing a line in the soil with a spade, occasionally digging up a small rock or tree root.

"How's it going, Dunc?"

Duncan lifted a hand from the shovel to signal a thumbs-up before again leaning on its handle to pierce the line into the soil. Cole lined up next to Duncan, wiggling his spade to the right position under the yellow line and jumping onto the knurled edges of the tool to break through the hardened soil.

"You need anything from me? If not, I'm going for a walk," Adam said more loudly. Duncan gave a slight wave and returned his hand to the spade.

⌒

It was only a half-mile from the house to the boulder. That's one of the reasons Adam had bought this house three years earlier when he got the CEO job—it offered a place to get away, get outside, burn off some stress, maybe teach his son, Jason, some rock climbing, and it gave

Maureen a place to putter around. Chicago was fine; in fact, other than New York or San Francisco, he could not have picked a better place to make it to the top. Still, there was nothing quite like getting outside in the mountains, the way he had during college.

He and Maureen loved the house at first sight. A rambling Arts and Crafts–style home, it was only five years old and had only one owner before them. It boasted exposed beams and expansive windows, with rambling stonework that left an impression that the house grew out of the rocky hillside behind it. Maureen adored the windows and the big kitchen; the skylights and the high ceilings gave you a feeling you were cooking and eating outdoors. The backyard was nothing much—a scrabble of stony soil with some patches of grass, scrub brush, sparse clusters of aspen trees, a few exposed rocks, and a porch and patio area that seemed a bit of an afterthought—but they were fixing all that now. Mo said she wanted to leave the backyard up to Adam since the kitchen was her preferred domain, but more than once she hinted to Adam that it would be nice to have some open space with grass so someday the grandkids would have a place to play without skinning their knees on the rocks. Sure, I'd like that too, Adam allowed himself, but I don't see that happening anytime soon. Jason's got some work ahead of him to find his own life before he takes on somebody else's.

Adam liked the fact that right outside their door and across a shallow arroyo were plenty of boulders to climb and, behind them, the first of a ridge of mountain cliffs. There was a palpable sense of mass and scale about the place that invigorated Adam; the way the stone mounds reared above the land around them spoke to ambition and imagination. Yet, he was also drawn to the solitude, the feeling that it was just him and the earth beneath him and the cliffs above him. When he was in the mountains, he felt small and large at the same time.

The walk from the house to the boulder had only taken about fifteen minutes on Friday, the day he fell; today, the walk took three times longer. Each step was draining, as the tips of the crutches found every pebble, every pocket of loose dirt, and every crack in the ground. By the time Adam reached the base of the boulder he was breathing heavily and his arms were quivering from holding the crutches. One thing for sure, he told himself—the next time I come out here, it will be without these crutches. Whatever it takes.

There was no cinematic moment in looking up at the rock that had wrecked his vacation, no sense of awe or fear. In fact, he was just ticked. That rock's not that big, he ruminated. I must have just been off my game that day. I'm not losing it. Accidents happen.

He sank his armpits into the padded tops of the crutches and just stood there, sagging, for what seemed like minutes. He pivoted gingerly against one crutch to lower himself to the rock table.

It was one of those mornings when the radiant heat of the sun was already slow-baking the thin air; the ground still glistened from a morning dew that had not yet fully burned off. The dirt and the stone gave off a mineral aroma that, to Adam, was bracing and fresh.

I love this whole deal, he thought, as he inhaled the mountain air.

The slight brush against his leg woke him up. He clawed away the fog in his head from the painkillers to make out the silhouette standing in front of him—a man tapping him on his knee with a walking stick.

"You okay?" the voice said.

"Um...yeah, fine." Adam reached for the crutches and tried to lever against one of them to get himself upright, but the rock seemed to sway beneath his feet.

"Easy. No rush," the man before him said, grasping Adam's upper arm.

Adam felt a little sheepish, falling asleep right out here in the open and then acting like some kind of drug-addled idiot. Well, he admitted, I am a little drug-addled.

"Do you know where you are?" the man asked him.

"Yes," Adam responded, more defensively than he meant to sound. "I live back behind that ridge."

"Okay, so you're not lost," the man said with a relieved voice. He thrust his hand forward to shake Adam's hand. "My name is Ajacopa, Ajacopa Calvo."

Adam returned the handshake as he ran the name through in his head a few times. "Can't say I've ever met anyone with a name like that."

"Well, now you have," the man smiled.

"Where are you from?" Adam leaned forward on his crutches, intrigued. "I mean, what country?"

"Peru."

Adam surveyed Ajacopa's clothes—hiking shorts, thick boots, a beige shirt with an insignia on the sleeve, a cap with an emblem in the center, a two-way radio lashed to his belt on one side, and a hunting knife pushed deep into a scabbard on the other—then spoke carefully.

"You don't look like a tourist."

"I'm a ranger," Ajacopa said, resting the heel of his hand on the knife's handle and looking back at Adam with a sly grin. "Don't worry, I only use that on mountain lions, and only when I fail to give them options other than to attack me."

Funny guy. Adam stared off across the arroyo for a few moments before turning his attention back to Ajacopa.

"Your name..." Adam shook his head, trying to clear the buzz. "I forgot it already."

"Ajacopa," he said. "Just call me A.J."

"A.J. Okay. Got it." Adam thumped his forehead with his knuckle, making light of his wooziness. "Funny, I've met other rangers out here, so you must be new."

"I was assigned this area a few months ago," A.J. said. "I'm glad to meet you."

Adam's ankle was throbbing again, so he eased himself back to a sitting position on the rock as A.J. leaned against the side of the boulder. The stone was cool against the back of Adam's legs and it seemed to salve the pain in his ankle.

"So, A.J.," he said. "You're a long way from home. Peru, huh?"

"I'm from a town called Arequipa," A.J. said brightly, patting his hand against his chest. "Always here in my heart, you know? Home..."

"Sounds like you miss it." Adam found himself intrigued by the stranger; if nothing else, the conversation was a refreshing counterpoint to the more restrained and cautious exchanges he'd had since becoming CEO. *Everybody takes me so seriously,* he would chuckle to himself. *It's still just me.*

"How long have you been in the U.S.?" he asked A.J.

"Almost ten years now," A.J. said slowly. "Too long."

"Why are you here? Why not go back? Sounds like you still care about the place," Adam said, dancing on the line between empathy and sympathy.

"Yes, I care about the place a lot," A.J. smiled nervously. "The problem is that for far too long I have cared too much."

Adam was baffled by the answer but felt the need to pull back a bit. He didn't want to intrude into what might be a deeply held story, and he was also wary of inviting a conversation longer than his aching body could tolerate.

"So," A.J. glanced down at the crutches and Adam's bandaged ankle, "what brings you out here?"

"Just getting out to stretch a bit and get some air." Adam gazed up at the rock, then let his eyes drift to the blue sky above.

"Really?"

Adam was usually quick with a comeback, but this time the words seemed to ball up somewhere in the back of his brain. It must be the pain pills.

"I don't know," he said quietly. "Funny, but I guess I'm not sure."

A.J. stood quietly, seemingly at peace with such a halting answer to the question. The seconds ticked by, but to Adam they felt like hours.

"Okay, that doesn't exactly give you the answer you were looking for, does it?" Adam broke the silence. He did not like feeling so unmoored, but even more, he did not like the feeling of vulnerability that was creeping in.

"I was just asking a question," A.J. responded reassuringly. "I'm not looking for any particular answer."

"Even so, I guess my answer is still the same—I don't know."

A.J. jumped the last few feet onto the path and turned back to face Adam. "Ah, there is so much we do not know! You are not alone, my friend." A.J. waved a good-bye before striding down the rocky trail and over the next crest.

Part II

———

AWARENESS

———

Four

———

"Did you see the voicemail on your cell?"

Maureen greeted Adam at the door before he had a chance to reach for the handle. Adam looked down at his cell phone and spotted the icon signaling the missed call.

"Shoot! Must have lost the signal when I was out at the rock."

"Shirley called here at the house when she couldn't reach you," Maureen said. "Something about the investment bankers needing to go over some issues, but Darren covered it since you were not available."

Adam tensed, then punched the speed dial button on the cell phone.

"Adam," Maureen said more firmly, "did you even hear me? Shirley said Darren took care of it."

If Adam heard her, there was no sign, as he pressed the phone to his ear and turned toward the bedroom.

It was nearly half an hour before Adam emerged. He sat down hard on the stool and rocked the cell phone on the counter for several seconds, finally laying it down and lacing his fingers behind his neck, glancing up toward the ceiling.

"Tough call, huh?" Maureen stepped away from the sink and leaned on the counter on both elbows, peering into Adam's weary face.

Adam encircled her hands in his and forced a smile.

"It's fine," he said, gamely. "It's just that everyone is a little wired right now."

Maureen retrieved her hands from his grip and now encircled his hands in her own.

"Like you're not?" She pressed his hands against her face and kissed his fingers, then turned back toward the sink. "Remember you're on vacation, buster."

After a few minutes of quiet, Adam pushed open the double doors to the patio and slumped into one of the lounge chairs. Maureen leaned out the door opening.

"Jason called, too," she said. "He's on break next week from classes and wants to come see you. He's trying to move his exam up now to get here sooner."

"That's nice, but he doesn't need to do that." Adam was leaning back now, closing his eyes against the midday sun. "I'm fine. Really."

"I think it would be good for both of you." Maureen's voice took on a gentler tone. "You both have a lot going on. Maybe you can compare notes."

Adam hesitated, unsure how to respond. He let the fatigue of the morning walk and the tension of the last hour sweep over him until the sounds and light of the day drifted away into the fog.

Whack!

Adam jerked awake, then almost as quickly slumped back into the chair, still weighed down by the weariness of the morning walk. The *whack* sound would not let him fall back asleep, so he eventually peered out from under heavy eyelids to see Duncan and Cole stacking more timbers near a pile of concrete bags.

There was a rhythm to the work; as physical as it was to move lumber, concrete, and steel, Duncan did it with fluid, measured movements, and Cole was mimicking that rhythm. No wasted effort, no needless exertion.

Adam guessed Duncan to be about fifty years old, but he had a sturdiness and agility about him that belied his age. He had a thick, muscled neck that seemed bolted onto his barreled chest and broad shoulders. Some people stay in shape because it shows they are disciplined; others stay in shape because it is the welcome consequence of their day job. As Adam watched Duncan, he was struck by the way everything Duncan did seemed so steady, almost easy. He could not tell if it was a pattern and rhythm born of repetition or out of the sheer simplicity of the work, but Duncan transitioned from one task to the next with the same measured pace.

Adam found himself strangely jealous. The job of a CEO—at least to its critics and in popular folklore— seems easy, Adam often ruminated. Nothing but cushy boardrooms, business lunches at the club, some assistant attending to the small things that loom large to those of lesser means. Nice vacation home. Stock options. Big severance package if you screw it up. All that.

Moving up the ladder for most of his career had been relatively easy for Adam—he just outworked everyone around him. As comfortable as he was with his talents, he knew he had a natural modesty and charm that kept critics at bay. His father used to tell him that nobody liked the smartest guy in the room; a little self-deprecation and humility goes a long way.

He also knew he wanted to be a CEO someday, and he readily embraced what it took to get there. Somehow, the honest quest to grow and the simple ambition to be the head guy seemed to blend over the years. There was an addictive energy about it all, knowing that the harder he worked, the more he was rewarded. It was a form of circular breathing, always moving, feeding on itself.

Adam knew better than to pretend his life was hard, but it did come at a price. One of those sacrifices was hard to accept: the possibility that he may have lost his younger brother Don along the way.

They hadn't had problems in middle school and high school—Adam recalled the pickup basketball games in the driveway, the late nights working on his car, the boastful talks about girls. He and Don were tight. No question.

I guess people can go different directions in their lives, Adam thought, but Don just seemed to go to another place altogether. He's the franchise owner of a small insurance office. Not that selling insurance is a lesser calling, Adam reminded himself, but it's disappointing that Don hasn't done more with his life. Maybe he could have purchased more franchises or taken a chance by raising and managing an investment fund. It just seems like he never had the ambition. He drives a six-year-old Ford Explorer. He and his wife, Anna, hardly ever take vacations; if they do, they rent a cabin in South Fork with another family and hang out the whole week barbecuing burgers, fishing at the lake, and playing nickel poker until midnight.

Adam remembers the times he and Don would take long drives through the country or just hang out at some sports bar, talking shop. But it seemed that every time Adam brought up an idea of what Don could be doing with his degree or sketched out a plan to get there, Don would bristle. Hard to know why, but Adam figured Don resented the fact that his older brother had moved so far ahead in his career. If that's the case, Adam asked himself, then why doesn't he let me help him?

Adam can't remember a reunion with Don in the last ten years that hadn't erupted into class warfare. Sometimes Don makes little digs, like commenting about Adam's Mercedes; other times, he launches a full frontal assault, telling Adam, "I'm surprised that Chicago zoning regulations allow you to ride around on your high horse." It hurts in a way that Adam chooses to never express— especially when he reminds himself that he put up his own money to help pay off Don's college loans after their dad lost his job. Later, Adam gave Don the money to help get the insurance office off the ground. No contract, no equity position, not even a handshake. Dad had said it would be good if I found a way to help Don get going, Adam thought, so I did, but it wasn't like he had to ask. I never asked Don to pay me back, but the fact that Don has never shown any appreciation for what I've done just feels wrong. On top of that, it's as though I'm not allowed to be his brother any more. That's what really hurts.

Jeanine's not that way but, then again, it's not like she and I talk much at all, Adam thinks from time to time. For a younger sister, she seems pretty settled. Not much money in nonprofit work, but she says she likes her *clients*. A little naïve, in Adam's mind, to call people who can't pay you half the time *clients*. But she likes it. At least she's not jumping on me all the time. Funny, she asks me how I'm doing and I tell her, but then she really never says much after that. Not sure if she doesn't know what to say, or does know and just doesn't want to. If we spent time with each other more often, he figures, it would be time well spent, because we just don't have that many expectations of each other.

The situation with Jason is, well, complex, Adam has decided. He's a good kid, really good. He has some growing up to do, and it seems to Adam that Jason is too ready to take off on his own before he really knows where he wants to go. Jason is stubborn, Adam rationalized, and there's only so much I can do to get him to listen. It just seems that Jason has trouble focusing on one thing at a time and is slow to go after opportunities that appear obvious. Adam tried to help; he remembers sitting down at the kitchen table time after time to help map out a development plan for Jason, to help him get more organized. More than that, Adam made calls—a lot of calls—to business contacts and others who he thought could help Jason or give him a foot-in-the-door job. It was frustrating; Adam would find out later that Jason did not always call them back or had failed to take the next step. As Adam saw it, Jason had squandered a lot of opportunities that Adam had built for him.

Over time, Adam's fatherly caution and Jason's dreams rammed into each other like two storm fronts in Kansas. Adam never felt he was trying to win the brittle arguments that came between him and his only child, but he hated feeling that he always came out the loser. Sometimes the exchanges were sour, other times acid. He'd lost sight of when the gentleness and playfulness between him and his son had gone away.

Adam remembers the sick feeling that washed over him the day that Jason left for California to go to photography school. Adam wanted to cheer him on—and outwardly he did—but in his gut he worried that it was a dead end. I want the best for Jason, Adam argued with himself, but maybe part of that is just letting him learn what it's like to fall flat on your face a few times so you can better appreciate that—most of the time—life asks more of you than it gives you.

I'm just trying to help. It's what I do, he assures himself from time to time.

And then, sometimes, he pays a price with Maureen. She's one of those people who just doesn't get all boiled up over every issue out there, although at times Adam thinks she avoids some that are worth getting a little ripped about. She takes a lot of stuff in stride and is almost always the one to come back first and give Adam a hug and apologize if they have a skirmish over something, but Adam suspects she swallows a lot of anger, too.

Adam still remembers the argument. For, as quiet as she is most times, this one came from somewhere deep. Maureen had complained that the conversations at the dinner table were turning into staff meeting reports, with Adam sizing up everyone and calculating the moves on the next deal. Adam just kept on rolling with his replay of the day, with its heroes and villains, its breakthroughs and disasters, while Maureen tried to get him on to some other topics. After a while, Maureen got quieter and quieter.

Then one day she exploded from the silence, wadded up a napkin, and threw it at him. She stood trembling behind her chair, as if she needed a shield, and said if this is what it is going to be like—all this work and tension and calculating and just worrying—she wished Adam would have chosen to be an insurance broker like his brother. Or a plumber. Or some guy who works in a warehouse.

Anything but a CEO.

At first, Adam was stunned, and even a little worried about what all that meant. His anger kicked in, at least later that night when Maureen had gone to bed alone and he had the kitchen to himself. Maybe she would feel differently, Adam argued to himself, if she did not have money to fly Jason all over the place, or the Lexus, or time and money to go to the club with her friends. Easy to say she would like to chuck it all, but she really doesn't know what that means.

Still, she seemed serious. "Where are you?" she had said.

It almost sounded rhetorical, it was that distant.

Five

____

What do you want?

The notepad was still on the patio table where Adam had left it, and Duncan's handwritten note was still at the top. Adam was hoping that by now Duncan would have filled out the page with more detailed sketches of the rest of the project, or at least some specific questions about dimensions and materials. Instead, the page remained blank.

"Okay." Adam said the word loud enough that Duncan looked up from his work.

"Okay, then," Adam repeated, grabbing the construction pencil on the table and stabbing at the paper, sketching out shapes with firm, fast strokes. The only sounds for the next few minutes were the scraping of Cole's shovel in the wheelbarrow and the splatter of water as Duncan held the hose over the concrete mix.

"I'm ready!" Adam put down the pencil and pushed himself out of the lounge chair, leaving the crutches behind as he hobbled triumphantly across the patio toward Duncan. "How's this?"

Duncan pushed his cap back and scanned the rough chart with the list down the side, then he handed the tablet back to Adam. "Well, okay, but I wonder if you might be disappointed."

Adam laughed nervously. "Well, I'm not an engineer, so maybe it doesn't look right, but that should be enough to get this thing going, right?"

"If all we are doing is figuring out how to start, sure. We can just get this done, meet the code, do the obvious," Duncan said with a careful tone, "or we could really make this something we can both be proud of for a long time."

"Like what?" Adam tried not to sound too impatient, knowing that projects like this have a way of spiraling out of control.

"We don't know yet," Duncan smiled. "Let's just work it a bit more, keep looking at it, keep our options open..."

"So, what do you want me to do?"

Duncan pushed the tablet back in front of Adam.

"Try starting with the end in mind." Duncan folded back the page with Adam's list, exposing a fresh, blank page. "Don't worry yet about how I'm going to do it. Just tell me what matters to you."

Adam picked up the pencil and held it poised over the paper. Just then, Duncan held his hand over the paper, blocking Adam's view.

"Take your time, Adam," he said. "Don't give in to the temptation to go too fast."

Duncan turned back to the wheelbarrow. Adam watched him work for a few minutes, as Duncan showed Cole how to fold the wet concrete into the next dose of dry mix so as not to stir up dust. Adam tucked the tablet under his arm, grabbed his crutches, and strode back toward the house.

"You look like a man on a mission." Maureen saw the resolve in Adam's posture as he lurched through the kitchen, but his face betrayed the confusion he still felt.

"Working harder than I thought I would," Adam said. Maureen shot him a puzzled look as he stroked his way into the den, flopped down on the leather couch, and started speed-punching the remote. He lifted his thumb for a few moments to catch the market report. Stocks in his sector were off a bit, mostly drifting lower awaiting the earnings reports over the next few days. No movement on his company, which was good. They had kept the acquisition talks tight. They did not need any rumors circulating that would get the other company feeling a little cocky about pumping up the price ahead of the definitive agreement negotiations. Run silent, run deep, Adam always cautioned himself in these deals.

The acquisition was the biggest in the company's history; in fact, it was also one of the very few in its history. Shortly after taking the job three years ago, Adam had walked the board through a classic build-or-buy strategic analysis of their market position and where the growth sectors would be in the next few years. Despite the company's strong culture to grow organically rather than extend itself into new markets, the board came around to Adam's view at the off-site two summers ago. He had worked hard to earn the board's confidence in his ability to put together something of this scale, and this was the payoff. Even though he relied on his natural confidence to press through something this big, he had to admit the strain had been wearing on him the last few weeks.

He couldn't complain of anything specific, just a gnawing sense that everything was on his shoulders.

He pressed down hard on the remote as the channels flickered by, easing up when it reached a sports channel.

Business is a game, he affirmed to himself as he watched the scores crawl across the bottom of the screen. Winners and losers.

And it's so nice to win.

⟡

Even with the volume turned low on the television, Adam barely heard the soft footsteps behind him on the den's oak floor. Maureen stood next to Adam at the couch, keeping her eyes on the television as she spoke. "The accident, the patio, going out to the rock so soon after your fall, on the phone to Chicago. When does your vacation start?"

Adam leaned back and looked up at her, reaching for her hand.

"Sorry, Mo," he said. "Overtaken by events. You're getting a chance to relax, though, right?"

"By myself, yes. But it's hard when you're not relaxing. What do I have to do—knock you out for days?" She laughed a bit nervously, but Adam caught the barb.

"I'll back off this next week—promise," he assured her, grabbing her hand and locking his fingers with hers. "I may go out to the rock and I do have to look over the porch work, but I'll try to steer clear of everything else."

She slipped away to the kitchen but was back just a minute later, easing down onto the couch next to him, handing him a cup of coffee and placing hers on the snack table in front of her.

"Okay, what's up?" Adam said.

"Nothing, Adam!" she said, failing to cloak the weariness she felt. "I'm just taking you up on the promise that we would find time to sit down together with a cup of coffee like we used to do..."

Adam let that one rest for a minute or two. They had suffered through this dialogue before, and it always seemed to fade out rather than reach a conclusion. Maybe it was because the end of that road felt like an intersection that only allowed you to turn one way or the other. They did not disagree—they both treasured their time together—but each day seemed to be busier than the last. It was as if they were both buying time now, trying to keep up with the pace of their lives in the hope that it might all break clear at some point. In Adam's mind, it did not help either of them to have this talk when there was little he could do to change the situation right now. It would just frustrate them both.

Having Adam in business school during their first year of marriage had been tougher than they thought. Mo's job at the hospital was not too demanding—mostly checking in patients and sometimes dealing with anxious family members in the waiting room—but the paycheck barely covered the basics of rent, food, and clothing. Adam hated the financial struggle even back then, but Mo never complained and said the business school investment was worth it if that is what Adam wanted to do. Adam remembers how pretty Mo looked even while wearing the cheap clothes from the outlet store—the only ones they dared buy—but he knew that other women kept score, and he wanted badly for her to not suffer the slights.

They had talked about having kids a year or two after Adam finished his MBA and got his footing in his career.

Maybe they should have been more careful, but Mo got pregnant while Adam still had a semester left to complete his degree. Adam landed a job in marketing in a well-respected company a few months after Jason was born. The job had a sizable bonus package, and within two years Adam was racking up some nice paychecks, enough to pay off the credit card balances they had run up during school and to let Mo buy some decent clothes.

"You don't have to keep working at the hospital if you don't want to," Adam had said one day when Jason was about two years old. "I think we'll be okay, but it's up to you."

"I want to be home with Jason," Mo had said, as if she had been waiting for his invitation.

Adam remembers the shocked look on her face when he told her a year later about the promotion into a promising sales territory and the move to Minneapolis. Adam thought it was an obvious decision—more money, a more stable situation for the family, good schools. He and Maureen had pledged to talk through decisions, especially the big ones, but this one seemed to overtake those good intentions. This is good for all of us, Adam assured Maureen; we can make new friends. He did not see her crying that night on the porch.

Adam won the top sales award for the company in his second year. Recruiters started calling. Minneapolis turned into Seattle and then, four years later, to his current company in Chicago. He started off as director of business development, a position with a pretty clear path to vice president, as his boss was just a few years away from retirement.

Adam was awash in his job and his growing duties; Mo was content to hold down the fort at home. Adam's position supported a comfortable home in the suburbs, with a decent yard for Jason and his friends, as well as good schools. Adam hoped that over time his salary increases would allow the family to move to one of the more upscale, gentrified neighborhoods in the city. Mo was always gracious when it came time to dress up for a business reception in the city, but she had little patience for the pretense and posturing she observed in the business and social elite at some of the functions. Most often, she could be found in the corner of the room having a playful and open talk with some other woman who was just as interested in kids and art as she was.

She seemed to like Chicago, though—at least she said she was happy for Adam as he took on more and more responsibility and, after a few years, was appointed senior VP of business development. What she did not expect was that Adam would come home four years later, telling her that the executive committee of the board was interviewing him as a potential successor to the CEO.

They both remember the conversation that night in the kitchen: What would it mean to be CEO? How much travel would there be? How many hours? How much entertaining would they have to do? Mo was very much at ease with herself and was not motivated to play up to a social circle, but she also knew that she had a role in Adam's public life at charity events and board retreats. They could do it, as long as they remembered the trade-offs they would each have to make to pull it off.

Adam had always been earnest in trying to keep a balance between his work and home life, but the goal was elusive. He made it to most of Jason's school events; he had to fight for space in his day to do it, and more than once he got to the school directly from work. But he made it. Put it on my calendar, and I'll be there, was Adam's commitment to himself and others. Somewhere in there he missed the spontaneous events, like the time Mo and Jason spent the whole day trolling antique shops in Old Town or seeing the photography exhibit at the art museum.

"You're back."

Adam did not have to turn around to recognize the voice. This was his first day without crutches, but he had grabbed a downed limb along his way to serve as a walking stick, in case his ankle was not yet up to the trek. At the sound of the voice, he twirled the stick in his hand to assure himself, as much as anyone, that he was recovering rapidly.

"How are you, A.J.?"

"Having a great day."

Adam smiled at that one. Pretty good gig—walking around outside all day, nobody picking at you. Can't imagine a bad day out here could be all that bad. Some days, he allowed himself, I wouldn't mind a job like this.

"Good," Adam said. "Glad it's working for you."

Adam stayed still, looking up at the rock for what seemed like several minutes, but he knew that A.J. had not moved either.

"So, why did you really come back today?" Somehow, Adam felt A.J.'s question was more probing this time than the first time he heard it.

"Okay, I guess I came back because, well...two reasons," he ventured. "First, yes, I wanted to get out here again and figure out why this rock knocked me on my butt when I've climbed it before. Second, I know I'll want to get back up there, and that won't happen if I shy away and distract myself with other things to do."

By now, A.J. had worked his way up the side of the stone table to stand beside Adam. They both surveyed the rock for several moments, A.J. looking at it curiously, Adam almost glaring at it.

"I don't know why I fell," Adam finally broke the stillness. "I've climbed that boulder before with no problem. It's not that tough a climb. Ticks me off, if you really want to know. It wasn't exactly my plan to spend half my vacation on crutches or a walking stick."

"No, but they do serve a purpose," A.J. chuckled, watching Adam trying to balance himself on the rock slab without bearing down too much on the bandaged foot sticking out through his hiking sandals. "But you're doing pretty well for just five days."

Now Adam turned to face A.J.

"How do you know when I fell?"

Just then, Adam noticed A.J. holding something out toward him. Even with the gouges and scratches, the striped and sculpted dome shape was instantly familiar. Adam reached out to take the climbing helmet, dusting it off, twisting it in his hands to detect any cracks, and running his fingers around the inside webbing.

"So, you were the one who found me."

"You were kind of out of it," said A.J. "It's my job anyway. That's one of the reasons I walk around here. There is usually somebody stuck somewhere, whether they know it or not."

Stuck.

Adam looked back at the rock with a fierceness that unveiled the confrontation that was boiling up in his mind.

"So, why do you think you fell, Adam?"

Adam shrugged his shoulders. "Hey, it just happened. Just an accident, I guess."

"Are you sure?"

I'm not, thought Adam, but sometimes that is the answer you have to give when you don't have a better explanation. I gave that same response to my dad whenever something was busted, he thought—when I pulled the car too far into the garage and hit the back wall, when I slept in one morning and missed my math final, when I blew my pass pattern in the all-state playoff game that led to the interception. It was the same answer I gave Maureen a year ago when she confronted me about what I blurted out after Jason told us he was going to Monterey for photography school. Sometimes you just make a mistake, and no matter how hard you search, there is no better answer.

"If you really want to know," Adam said more slowly. "I came here today because I was hoping I might get up the face of this a few feet, you know, just to see. Crazy, huh?"

"Well, you have a sprained ankle, a concussion, you're tired—and you came out here to climb the rock," A.J. folded his arms against his chest and turned to face Adam. "You always play hurt?"

"No...well, yeah," Adam felt a little defensive. "You don't always have a choice. Sometimes it goes with the job."

"Adam," A.J. unfolded his arms and looked at his watch. "What are you doing this afternoon?"

"Nothing," he said, surprised that A.J. seemed to have shifted the conversation. "I'm on vacation. Just playing general contractor for our backyard project, trying to get some things moving in the right direction at the office, watching ESPN." His voice revealed sadness more than any hard edge. "Some vacation, huh? Why?"

"I have to check some campsites across the canyon now, but I'll be back around this way about four o'clock," A.J. said. "Since you're grounded anyway, maybe we can swap some climbing stories."

"Sure, I guess." Adam was hoping one of the stories would not be a retelling of his fall. "I'll see how the day goes."

⌒

When Adam got back to the house, he checked his cell phone for messages. There was one, from Shirley.

"Adam, Mort called." Shirley's voice was steady, as always, but he could hear the flicker of stress in her tone. "He needs you to call him right away. He said to have the last 10Q with you when you call. I just e-mailed it to you so you would have it."

What's up with that? Adam wondered. In Adam's estimation, Mort was something of a church mouse as a board member, hardly one to initiate anything. Adam had him pegged as a legacy, old-school board member. He was a golfing buddy of Chuck, the previous chairman and CEO; Adam was pretty sure they still paired up for eighteen holes now and then.

Mort was a "twofer," not just a journeyman board member but a member of the finance committee and the executive committee. Adam was respectful toward Mort but did not worry much about him, given that Mort was always quiet in board meetings, mostly listening and sometimes asking a question or two that seemed off-topic or just *different*. He had owned a large regional real estate company, and seemed to have been on the board forever. There were times when Adam wondered whether the company would be better served by having a fresh person in that board seat, but Mort did no harm—and Adam felt confident that Mort would vote on his side.

"Hi, Mort...Adam. You needed me to call?" Adam had the 10Q open on his tablet on the kitchen table and had already refreshed himself on the numbers before making the call. He leaned back in the chair to relax himself, but he had to admit he was not finding a comfortable position.

"Sorry to bother you on vacation, Adam," said Mort. "I just wanted to give you a call and see if we could talk through a few things that I think might come up with the investment bankers. It's mostly around your two acquisitions last year. I thought it would help if you could refresh me a bit on when we were expecting them to hit the break-even point."

Interesting that Mort called them *my* two acquisitions, Adam noted. In reality, it was true. Adam had only been CEO for a few months before he started putting some small acquisition targets in front of the board. It was his strategy to test the board's collective stomach for such deals, but it was also to test the strength of the company's brand and market position after so many years of relative complacency under Chuck. They were not big acquisitions—mostly filling in some product and distribution gaps and nosing the company into niches that would have been too costly to cut into on their own. Still, equity analysts took note of the moves and did some nice write-ups about Adam's more ambitious strategy.

"I don't think you have a reason to be concerned," Adam responded reassuringly to Mort's questions. Adam never got into a lot of detail with Mort, figuring that laying out details was out of place, given that Mort had usually deferred to Chuck's judgment in these things and Adam was hoping for the same kind of deference now. "Yes, we thought the acquisitions would be accretive to earnings by now, but you know some of the transition issues that popped up. We at least have the trend line going in the right direction. Why?"

"Well," Mort said slowly, "it's just that those acquisitions are a bellwether for the investment banks. They are not getting a clear signal about how we would handle a bigger deal right now. Some of us are worried that the analysts might have the same questions."

"Mort, I think it would make sense to remind them that we got a ten percent kick on stock price from those deals and never had to give it back," Adam countered. "The market gets it. They know the position we now have. Frankly, I think we have some investment bankers playing bean counters."

"Well, that's their job on these things, too," Mort replied. "I just would like you to step back a bit and take a fresh look at some of the conditions we are facing. I've consulted with Beth and we agreed to ask Darren to sit in on a finance committee meeting with the bankers tomorrow afternoon..."

"No," Adam jumped in. "I need to be there. I'll fly in."

"It's your vacation, Adam. You don't need to be here. We can do it by phone . . ."

Adam made an effort to tamp down his rising defensiveness. Be cool, he reminded himself.

"I appreciate that, Mort, but really—I need to be there. I'll cover it."

Adam pushed out a breath through pursed lips. I sounded a little edgy there, he scolded himself, but I'm not about to lay down with so much at stake. Plus, he had to admit some of the edge came from the mention of Darren.

Darren was five years older than Adam. Shorter, balder, with a second-tier MBA degree, and—at least in Adam's opinion—lacking an ambitious enough view of the market for the CEO job. Darren got stuff done as COO; more than once he had carried the water for Chuck. He had done the same later for Adam, taking the hit for some layoffs they had to make in one division and carving out favorable contracts with suppliers. If we were in a war, Adam assured himself, I would want Darren in the bunker with me. Maybe I wouldn't want him crafting the war strategy, but he can carry it out better than most.

Adam had assumed that Darren was a Chuck guy, but at the very first staff meeting under Adam, Darren appeared to dig right in on the forward plans. He and Adam were not close; there was no "Hey, let's grab lunch" moments or golf games, but Darren seemed to be loyal to the strategy, if not particularly loyal to Adam himself. Still, when it involved the board, Adam saw Darren perk up and, more often than not, offer to step up.

Adam never got the inside scoop on whether Darren had been on the short list for CEO, or if Darren even wanted the job at the time. Adam did not want to squeeze him out; he needed an operations guy like Darren on the team. Please don't drive the business, Darren, he thought to himself. Just run it.

Six

––––

A.J. was already at the rock, looking out across the arroyo, when Adam came up the path, still stepping gingerly on his bandaged foot, making little use of the walking stick that dragged at his side.

"You're back!" A.J. said. "How's it going, Adam?"

Adam rolled his eyes and lowered himself to a sitting position a few feet from A.J.

"Where do I begin?" he groused, scuffing at the ground. He followed A.J.'s gaze and stared out across the arroyo. The late afternoon sun was painting the cliffs in amber and caramel hues; angular shadows stretched across the tables of rock as the sun slipped toward the horizon.

"Anything you want to talk about?" A.J. asked, without looking over at Adam.

"Can't," Adam said. "At least some of it I can't."

"The other...?"

Adam kept his gaze out across the canyon.

"Don't want to, really..."

Adam expected A.J. to fire off another question, but nothing came. The heat that had soaked into the rocks during the afternoon now radiated from the rock ledge beneath him. The sundowner winds started to kick up, brushing his face with cooler air that at least served as a counterpoint to the headache he felt bearing down on him.

"I've got a headache," he blurted out.

A.J. laughed. "I can see that."

"No," said Adam sharply, turning toward A.J., "I mean a *headache* headache. This day just unwound. I've got this guy doing some work at the house and he keeps asking me a lot of questions rather than just doing the work, and then I've got a bunch of bankers back at the office who are second-guessing our financials, and my wife wants me to relax, and then my son comes all the way out here even though I've got so much coming at me right now I can't do much with him. I'm days into my vacation and it doesn't exactly feel like one..."

"Adam!"

"What?!"

"Take a breath." A.J. bore in on Adam. "I'm serious. Take a breath."

Adam's next breath was more like a quick gust. A.J. stepped back a pace and placed his palms on his own chest.

"No, like this, my friend," he said, allowing his rib cage and shoulders to lift with a deep inhale and letting the air ease out over several seconds.

Adam followed his lead, but it was an awkward, forced attempt. "I'm sorry, I've just got a lot going on," he said. "I like activity, but not when there appears to be so many moving parts."

"So, are you one of the moving parts?"

Adam fell silent for a few seconds, reaching down to scratch his bandage, but not because it itched. I don't know, he thought. Action is good; moving—moving ahead—is an ability and a discipline that many people lack. He had it, he assured himself.

"Maybe," he finally said, shaking himself out of his thoughts. "What's wrong with that?"

"Nothing, I suppose," A.J. said, "if all that activity is accomplishing something."

"You are either moving forward or you are slipping back."

"You believe that?"

"Absolutely."

"Okay," said A.J. slowly. "I'm not here to challenge what you say, just to understand what you mean. So let me ask you something: What is your definition of 'moving forward?'"

"You know—improving, expanding, growing, not getting complacent with where you are."

A.J. smiled and leaned toward Adam.

"Faster?"

"Faster."

"And what about *slower*?"

"You're kidding, right?" Adam fought hard not to laugh. "What does slower get you?"

"Sometimes slower is faster."

"Look, slowing down is what I do on weekends or vacations," Adam smiled wryly at the irony of his own statement, realizing the growing tension he was feeling about the events in Chicago. "If I slowed down at work, I would get killed. If anything, I need a few people around me to speed up, not slow down."

"Is that what you were doing when you fell—speeding up?"

Adam was a little taken aback by the question. "It's not the first time I've climbed it."

"So you think it was just an unfortunate accident."

"I suppose so. Accidents happen, A.J., and I just happened to get caught on the wrong end of the deal this time."

A.J. strode up the shallow grade to the base of the boulder. "Do you mind showing me where you were on the boulder when you fell?"

The memory was painfully fresh. Adam stood close to the rock and used both hands to sketch out his route.

"I started here, pretty much went straight up to that crease, then I angled over here, anchored my feet there—and right there is where..."

Adam had turned around and realized he was talking to himself. A.J. was nowhere to be seen.

"Hey, A.J.!" Adam called out. "Where'd you go?"

"Down here!" A.J.'s voice could be heard through a scrub of saplings down and to the right of where Adam stood. "Don't worry, I can still hear you."

"But you can't see from down there," Adam said.

"Actually, you can," A.J. replied. "C'mon down. I'll show you."

Adam eased himself off the rock table and limped down the path to where A.J. was gazing up at the rock, now bathed in a wash of amber and rust from the setting sun.

"I'm not sure what you want me to see," Adam shrugged. "I think I know the surface pretty well."

"Adam, try not to think so much," A.J. said, resting his hand on Adam's shoulder. "Just look. Tell me what you see."

It became a challenge in Adam's mind at that point, like finding a secret number disguised in a drawing. He scanned the surface for several seconds, mentally cordoning it off into segments and carefully scrutinizing the surface.

"Anything different?" A.J. stood next to him.

"No..." Adam said slowly, still conducting his scan of the surface. "Wait, there! The rock is sheared off," Adam finally said in triumph, as he pointed toward a section just above where he got stuck. "There used to be a handhold there. That's where I was searching with my hand when I fell. The handhold is gone!"

A.J. stood next to him, with his arms folded across his chest, smiling broadly.

"I was thinking it was there," Adam admitted. He stepped back and grunted. "Can't believe I missed that."

"You can't think and be aware at the same time, Adam. You see it now because you slowed down long enough to see it differently." A.J. said. "Plus, it's later in the day, so the sun falls on the surface at a better angle. That's all."

A.J. studied Adam's face for several moments.

"I was a tour guide on the Inca Trail in my old country," A.J. said proudly. "There is much to see, but too many tourists just wanted to prove how fast they could walk the trail and get to Machu Picchu. We had two guides, and often I would take the forward position so I could intentionally walk slowly to make sure everyone behind me slowed down and actually took in all the beauty," he said impishly. "They used to call me *El Lento*—the slow one, but my tour groups always got the best photos!"

A.J. stood up, waved a farewell to Adam, and started to melt into the shadows of the path as Adam called out to him, "I'm off to Chicago in the morning. Back on Friday."

"That's a quick trip," A.J.'s voice cut through the darkness. "Don't have an accident!"

Seven

The CEO change three years ago had come earlier than some had expected. Earnings had improved and had held steady through the last three years under Chuck. Still, a more detailed analysis showed that the earnings performance was largely the result of productivity improvement programs and some tuning up of logistics and key supplier arrangements. Loose change, Adam would think to himself when he sat in on Chuck's quarterly report to the board. It was more cost control than revenue growth, and they were running out of ways to cut their way to success. With the high rate of internally generated capital and cash on hand, I could really kick this thing into a new gear if they gave me a shot at it, Adam daydreamed in the meetings.

Over time, a growing number of board members began wondering whether Chuck was playing not to lose, rather than playing to win. In particular, Beth Donato, head of the finance committee, would barely disguise her fidgeting when Chuck kept talking about "indexed growth" as a way to explain the company's slow but sure slippage in its rankings. She had carved her own path in the Chicago business jungle twenty years earlier, starting as a junior market relationship manager within her family-owned bank. Over a few short years, she was put in charge of market development, where she headed an initiative to roll up several smaller community banks into a regional powerhouse that soon was behind some of the largest commercial development and mergers and acquisitions dealmakers in town. Adam never asked her how she did it; she just did it, and maybe that's what mattered.

Everyone knew she made a fortune when the family sold the business to one of the big national banks, and there was a lot of speculation about what she might do with her newfound wealth. So it was a surprise when she popped up publicly on only a few community projects. The only board seat she kept was with Adam's company. She had built her career pushing for tough targets and working hard to achieve them, even as a board member, so Adam figured the board seat was her way of staying in the game. Beth was tough, gutsy, and to the point; Adam counted her as a kindred spirit. Some people in the company and the business community even credited or accused her of putting together a coalition to depose Chuck and install Adam.

Adam was confident that he had an able ally and a trusted advisor in Beth. He also had calculated that Beth could move the votes with two other members of the finance committee. Given that two finance committee members were on the executive committee as well, Adam knew where and with whom he could best apply leverage without appearing to make a direct play for Chuck's job.

Whatever took place behind the scenes, Adam knew that the way he conducted himself in front of the whole board was what would count the most. It wasn't selfish ambition, Adam told himself. I've got a stake in this thing too, and if I'm showing I've got what it takes to drive it, that's in everyone's interests.

Adam believed in the strategic advantage of swinging for the fences on an early pitch, or going long on third and short: surprise the other side. Don't make the obvious move or you'll be suckered. You don't know what you can do unless you try, and you can't wait for ideal conditions to try. That was his philosophy. Sure, he had miscalculated earlier on some contracts—the big major-league hitters have many more strikeouts than they do homers—but the homers are game changers. Adam had taken the view that it was better to take a shave on margins up front on a few deals, knowing that the company would work the opportunity over time to wring out the earnings. You have to land the deals—buy some strategic market share and build the brand—or you'd never get a chance to do anything. That is the way Adam saw it. Prompted by some discussions that began in the finance committee, the board seemed to come to the same point.

It had to be hard for some of them to broach the issue of retirement with Chuck, especially since he had brought on several of the board members and was practically a legend at the company. Oddly, Chuck seemed to be ready for the conversation, certainly in no mood to balk. Adam thought it was an easy decision for someone like Chuck to make; after all, the old man had a fat severance package, buckets of deferred compensation, and full vesting, right when the stock was still trading at a decent level.

Chuck did not want to stay on the board as a non-executive member; under the circumstances, he probably could have if he had pushed it, but he wanted to get out of the way. Plus, he knew himself well enough to realize that he would bristle every time someone brought up the modest revenue trend line, and he did not want to be the elephant in the room if and when the board needed to make some tough decisions to change course.

The board chairman, Stan Marshall, had been brought on a few years earlier when there was a big governance push to separate the CEO and board chairman positions. It was a good fit. Stan had plenty of his own businesses to run and was not competing for the helm of Chuck's company. Plus, Stan, who was a member of both the executive and finance committees, was known by the analysts and the institutional investors, and had the kind of bank and club relationships in town that would go a long way in providing further gravitas if the company ever needed to draw on those kinds of reserves.

One of the board members had broken radio silence and told Adam that the executive committee vote naming him as CEO had been unanimous. Still, Adam was uncertain about where he stood with Mort, especially after that brief hallway conversation following the executive committee vote. Adam had walked up to Mort, mostly out of courtesy, and thanked him for his support. Mort said something like, "I did what I had to do." That's an odd comment, Adam thought at the time. Not exactly the ringing endorsement and adulation that had marked most of Adam's early career.

Adam was restless as the airplane curled up into the crystal blue Colorado sky. As soon as the plane leveled off, he flipped open his laptop and called up the latest acquisition brief. He pulled the small notebook from his briefcase and sketched out some points he wanted to make in his talk with Mort and the finance committee that afternoon. Still, it felt weird that Mort called him at all; it sounded like a heads-up call, but that would not be Mort. Maybe Mort was trying to scare him off the deal for some reason? Maybe Mort was freelancing this one and had his own agenda? So, he calls me on vacation, Adam pondered as he stuffed the laptop back into its case and pushed back the seat to recline.

Something's up.

Adam grabbed a quick lunch on his way from the airport and was at the office by one o'clock. Shirley was waiting for him.

"How's the foot?" she asked, looking down for a bandage or brace.

"Like steel. Back on it in two days," Adam said, rooting some files out of his briefcase and stacking them on the side of her desk. "Okay, three days, maybe."

"And your head?"

Adam smiled and tapped his brow with his forefinger. "Iron."

"Pig iron?" They both laughed as Adam started toward his office.

"Mr. Lawrence is already in your conference room," Shirley said quietly. "He got here half an hour ago. Remember, the finance committee meeting is at two o'clock."

Adam stepped through the doorway to his office, tossed his briefcase on the desktop, and turned toward the adjoining conference room. Mort was drinking a cup of coffee and browsing through some trade journals. He was a small man, roundish, and looked even more so when swallowed up in the tall and wide leather chairs that surrounded the conference table. His tight, curly hair was grayish red, thinning on top. For an attorney at a venerable old-money firm downtown, Mort was surprisingly disheveled. He rarely wore a tie, and the shirts and slacks he wore were more comfortable than crisp. He had black-rimmed glasses that he often slipped on and off his face in what appeared more to be a nervous tic than a need to adjust his vision near or far. He had a thin, strained voice that too often sounded like he was excited, yet everything else about him suggested ambivalence, no matter how intense the issue or discussion. He was so unassuming, Adam sometimes joked that he took it for granted that Mort was in board meetings even when he was absent.

Adam felt a bit ashamed of himself when he slipped into those kinds of remarks about Mort, because he was actually sympathetic toward him, and he figured the rest of the board felt the same way. Mort was a living legacy at the company, predating even Chuck's appointment as CEO fifteen years earlier. It was hard to imagine a time when Mort could not be seen shuffling in each quarter, leaving his box of saltwater taffy on Shirley's desk for her to put in her candy jar in the reception area, and taking his regular seat halfway down the table for the meetings.

Mort and his wife, Barbara, were childless and were not very visible in the Chicago business hub, so everyone was taken by complete surprise the day that Mort said he would have to miss the next board meeting or two to take care of his wife. He simply said it was ovarian cancer, and never got into the details of her illness.

Everyone sent flowers and cards to Mort when they got the final word, but there was no mention of a funeral or memorial service. Mort just showed up at the next board meeting, dropped off his candy, and quietly took his seat. All the board and executive team members came up to him single file, put a hand on his shoulder, and whispered to him, and he responded as he always did, with a gentle smile and a nod.

He wanted to stay on the board, and everyone from Stan on down agreed he was good to have as a member, that it would be an insult to even suggest it was time to move on.

"Don't get up . . ." Adam waved at Mort as he reached across to shake his hand and turned toward the chair at the head of the table.

"Only if you sit down, then."

Adam was oddly taken off guard by the good-natured poke at his accidental fall, and brushed aside an impulse to analyze the comment.

"So," Adam felt most comfortable when he could direct the discussion, especially given that Mort rarely did, "I went over the revenues on all the divisions. All above plan. I think we are in good shape." Adam chided himself for coming out of the blocks so fast and hard. It would have been more strategic to just lay back and get Mort to talk, to smoke out whatever was on Mort's mind.

Mort sat back in the chair and reached for his coffee. "I hear the bankers are trying to get a read on our capacity for an acquisition of this size," Mort looked down as he talked, fingering the pages of one of the journals.

"I can understand that," Adam policed his impulse to make a case before it was needed. "What are they concentrating on?"

"How we have managed the acquisitions we have done so far..." Mort let his voice trail off, leaving his statement as a dangling question.

"So, is there an issue there?"

"Well, you know, even those of us on the board were taken by surprise that both acquisitions had some rough patches initially that did not show up in due diligence. We just need to make sure we have our eyes and ears open on this one."

"Mort, I know you can appreciate that it is hard to uncover stuff that the other party is determined to hide." Adam tried to stay calm, but this felt like an assault on his competence. "Due diligence is just that—diligence. It's not perfection."

"I understand that," Mort pushed back the chair and stood up, looking casually out the window as he spoke. "Adam, I know I'm not one to speak up often. But I do observe a lot. And when I see something that I think others miss I'm not going to let it go by without calling it out."

"With all respect, Mort, I have thought this through pretty thoroughly," Adam said with calculated conviction. "I'm not aware that I'm missing anything."

"We never are, are we," Mort said almost too quickly for Adam to hear. Mort turned to face him. "You're moving pretty fast..."

"Mort," Adam was back on his feet, "remember that the strategy was to drive top-line growth and get established in the market. Those were my marching orders when I took this job, and I have kept the board in the loop on that at each board meeting and off-site. Nobody ever said that earnings would be the focus this early. We still have transition and start-up expenses to burn off."

"I know, Adam," Mort braced his hands on the table. "Things change, though. Have you taken some time to talk with the rest of the board? I think it would help you get a better sense of their concerns."

"I have talked with the board, Mort. Every meeting."

"You have presented the plans, Adam, but I mean have you gotten a read of your own on the board's thinking?" Mort sat back in the chair to see if the gesture could ease some of the brewing tension. "Adam, I don't for a moment doubt your intelligence or your energy. In fact, that is the issue—I am afraid you may be overthinking the board's concerns and questions instead of just stepping back a bit and seeing the situation from their perspective."

Adam strode over to the set of windows farther down the wall from where Mort sat, sweeping the blinds aside with his fingers. "Mort, with your history, you know as well as anyone that we needed to take this company up a notch, get back in the game. I feel like I'm doing that, and I fully appreciate that there is some stress in that. But over the past few weeks it seems like someone is changing the playing field."

"Adam, it's nothing personal," Mort said, but his tone was firming up. "Everyone knows what you've done, but we have to be careful. We can't afford a mistake."

The mistake is second-guessing ourselves when it gets a little tight and tough, Adam thought. The first two acquisitions were a shakedown cruise; there are always some bumps when you haven't done M&A as a matter of course. It's time to step up, yet when things get a little scary or risky, the board pulls back to where it was with Chuck, hunkered down as the market moves away from us. That kind of hesitation and aversion to risk is what got us into trouble in the first place. I can't let them go back...

"Mort, we need this deal." Adam caught his rising pitch, so he sat down to come across as more measured, but he still felt his frustration bubbling up. "I have moved the needle more than once in getting us the market share we wanted. The next level up has to be this acquisition. It's perfect for us—the right market, the right product set, the price is good."

"But, Adam, the board just wants to make sure..."

"We're too far down the pike at this point to start worrying about a bunch of 'what-ifs' that due diligence has told us are unlikely," Adam appealed. "We'll just distract ourselves. This deal is the one. We just have to make it work. It's too important."

"To whom?" Mort knew the question would bite, so he intentionally leaned back in his chair, taking off his glasses and hoping Adam would not feel an attack. His strategy failed.

"What's *that* supposed to mean?" Adam stood up and leaned on his knuckles over the polished wood surface of the conference table, his eyes glazed in barely suppressed anger. "If this deal isn't right, I'll be the first one to say we need to step away."

"I'm not asking you to step away from the deal," said Mort. "We just need you to slow down, step back, and make sure we look at this from all angles."

Sometimes slower is faster.

Adam sensed that the words he first heard from A.J. at the rock had a place in what was becoming a testy exchange with Mort, but he couldn't stop to consider them at the moment. Right now, he thought, I have to settle this or it's going to spin out of control.

"I have done everything you and the board asked of me. I never imagined you and others wouldn't stand behind this—and me." Getting personal in a business debate was something Adam prided himself in avoiding, but he had to pull out the stops to halt any momentum behind Mort's concerns. "I thought, Mort, I could count on your support for this deal. Instead, it feels like you are trying to kill it."

"No," Mort said, as he planted his glasses back on his nose, stood up, and walked to the middle of the room, "I'm trying to help you...if you will let me. But you're making it hard on everyone. Including yourself."

Adam looked away toward the window, trying to find the right words. He was still staring out the window when he heard Mort's soft footsteps on the carpet and the click of the conference room door closing behind him.

At first, Adam was lost in a swirl. He had to stick up for himself and what he was trying to do. Still, he wondered if he was so intent on winning that he left Mort feeling the loser. This wasn't supposed to be a battle, he agonized to himself; I thought the whole idea was that the board would respect the work I've put into this and at least follow my lead—certainly scrutinize, but not pick apart the basic underpinnings of the strategy. Now I've turned Mort into a loose gear, one who might tell people I'm bullying this thing through. Stupid. I should have just worked it through with him like Chuck always did. At least keep him on my side. He's not a player on the board, but I wonder if I just burned a bridge.

To Adam, all the work he'd put in to gain the confidence of the board on his plans for growth and all the goodwill he felt he had stocked up over the last two years driving good results seemed to have turned to vapor. As he gazed down the empty expanse of the conference table, he could not escape it.

For the first time in his career, he felt alone.

⸻

"Mort, we're running out of time." Stan trusted Mort more than anyone, but his impatience was showing. He had waved Mort into the kitchen area of the boardroom so they would be out of eyesight and earshot of the other board members, who were streaming in for the afternoon session.

"I'm talking with him, Stan," Mort said firmly. "I just need to get him to slow down a bit."

"I like confident, determined people, Mort, but there is a point where it crosses over into stubbornness," Stan hissed. "I'm not about to stand aside and see this go into a ditch."

"Stan, we need to remind ourselves that we created some of this," Mort rested his hand on Stan's shoulder. "We told him to come in here and make something happen, and he's doing that."

"Well, we can't afford to have him get deal heat…"

"He knows that, Stan. Just imagine how he feels—he probably thinks we pulled the rug out from underneath him. If we have a problem here, we are part of the problem."

Stan looked out toward the room where most of the attendees were taking their seats.

"I'd feel a whole lot better if he would just step back a minute and get our reactions," Stan said, controlling his simmering impatience. "I'm not going to let us get run over. He needs to remember we support him, and stop acting like we don't."

"I think I can get him there, Stan," Mort said. "Let me talk with him again. If I can just get him to trust me a bit, I think we can have the conversation you need us to have."

Adam was heading down the hallway toward the board-room when he heard the familiar voice behind him.

"Hey, that's not much of a limp for a guy who likes to jump tall boulders at a single bound!"

Adam turned and smiled broadly at the woman walking toward him.

"The rock took the worst beating, Beth. Good to see you."

Beth stood before him, clasping a notebook in front of her with both hands and looking up at him with a slightly concerned look.

"Seriously, you okay? You worried us."

"Yeah, I'm fine," he said dismissively. He felt strangely wary in his response. Beth was in his corner, but Adam had her pegged as being all business. So, it was best to keep it on that level and not risk assuming some personal regard that may not be there. Adam felt his footing coming back as he changed the subject.

"So, what are we looking at?" Adam tossed a glance toward the boardroom door.

"Let's save that for the meeting, Adam," she said gently but firmly. "Best to talk through anything there so we stay together on this. Meantime, please take it easy. We have all hands on deck for the deal, so don't row this on your own. We're here to help, okay?"

Adam stepped aside graciously to let Beth take the lead into the boardroom. As he entered behind her, he greeted everyone around the table individually. He worked his way toward his seat at the conference table, taking a head count of the bankers and board members. Darren slipped up behind him and spoke in a hushed tone:

"Mort asked me to be here in case there are some questions about operations," he said. "Up to you if you want me to stay or if you want to handle it..."

Adam barely heard him. His eyes were riveted on the doorway from the kitchen where Mort was walking out with Stan. Adam was kicking himself. This was not the plan. His job was to keep this deal moving, and he should not have to worry about which board members were on his side.

One thing he knew for sure.

Mort wasn't. And now maybe Stan wasn't, either.

"How was your flight?" Maureen was cutting some roses near the front flowerbed but stretched upright brightly when Adam pulled into the driveway and came up the front walk.

"Fine, I guess," he said dispiritedly. "On the surface, I thought the meeting with the bankers went well, but I'm afraid Mort's backpedaling on me."

"Mort?" Maureen asked gently. "He's pretty supportive."

"I know, I don't get it," Adam said, in almost a pleading tone. "Mort's starting to slow this thing down. What's worse, I think he's working behind my back to undermine this deal with Stan and the rest of the finance committee. I never said he was courageous, but I always thought he had my back."

Mo was always careful not to delve into Adam's board relationships, but she saw the stern look on Adam's face. "I've only met him a few times at board retreats and holiday parties, but he seems like a pretty decent guy..."

"Yeah, he is. That's why I can't figure out why he was coming at me so hard on this. I'm not sure if he felt that way himself or if he's allowing himself to be someone's messenger. Either way, I'm not feeling like I can trust him now."

Maureen pinched Adam's chin between her fingers and looked at him carefully.

"Are you sure?"

Adam sighed and reached for her hand, pressing it against his face. "No, I'm not sure. After this week, I wonder if I'm seeing anything correctly."

Maureen brushed some potting soil off of her hands and kissed Adam playfully on the lips.

"Glad you're home," she said. "There's a nice surprise for you inside."

Part III

ACCEPTANCE

Eight

Adam hoisted the carry-on over the threshold of the front door and dragged it behind him as he walked toward the kitchen. As he came around the corner, he spied the signs right away—the canvas backpack, the baseball cap, and the water bottle tossed on the counter.

"Hey."

Adam turned to the sound of the voice. Jason was walking in from the den, hands in his pockets, his eyes casting a glance downward as Adam rolled his foot to ease the cramp from the flight.

"You okay?"

"Yeah," said Adam, stepping forward stiffly at first. Then he relaxed, smiled, and wrapped his arms around his son, thumping the back of Jason's shoulders with his open palms. He stepped back and sat down on one of the stools in the kitchen. "Just a sprain and a mild concussion. I'm fine. You?"

"Fine."

They both seemed to size each other up for a few seconds, Jason inspecting his father's posture and face for signs of unacknowledged pain, Adam holding a poker face as he took in the scene of Jason's scuffed sandals, his black T-shirt, and his worn jeans.

"How's school?" Adam broke eye contact, turning to a kitchen cabinet to seek out a glass.

"I'm really liking it," Jason brightened. "I totally nailed my courses on natural light and composition. I did not do as well with the studio portrait class, but that's not really the direction I want to go anyway."

"I guess I didn't think about all the different directions you might go with photography," Adam said. "I just assumed you would have to be a jack-of-all-trades to make a living at it, at least at first." Adam jammed the glass under the fresh water spout on the refrigerator.

Jason spoke up over the sound of the water swirling into the glass.

"I like being back here," Jason said carefully, determined to get the conversation back to a more comfortable area.

"I'm glad to hear that," Adam braced his arms on the counter and looked down, as Jason started to drift toward the den. "How long will you stay?"

"We'll see how it goes. I won't wear out my welcome— promise." Jason called back over his shoulder after slumping down onto the couch and restarting a movie with the remote.

"It's great to have you here, you know that. I just don't want you to feel like you have to take too much time away from your classes." He waited a few seconds to see if Jason might respond, but he only heard the music and voices coming from the TV. Adam walked back to the bedroom, rolling his carry-on luggage behind him.

He traveled so often that packing and unpacking was a quick, almost thoughtless, routine. This morning, he took his time, ambling back and forth from the laundry basket to the chest of drawers, relishing the quiet and the chance to regroup after the Chicago discussions. He replayed the conversations several times in his mind—the awkward talk with Mort, Beth's pleasant greeting that turned colder when he asked for insights into the board's mood, and the hushed conversation in the back of the boardroom between Mort and Stan. It was hard to piece together.

Let it go, he told himself as he pulled on some shorts and a T-shirt, and bent down to lace his hiking boots.

Wind it down. You're on vacation.

He came out to the kitchen and absentmindedly sorted through some mail that Maureen had left for him. After a few minutes, he got up, seeing Jason still immersed in the movie, and headed for the back door.

"If you're going out," Jason's voice came out from the other side of the couch in the den, "you might want to talk to your guy Duncan. Some problem came up."

Adam walked past the patio and navigated around some mounds of dirt and rock to where Duncan was spearing a shovel into the ground. With each effort, the shovel sprang back up with a dull *clank*. Cole stood next to him with a can of spray paint, squeezing the nozzle at each point where Duncan met resistance.

"Hey, Dunc!" Adam called out, "Need a shovel sharpener?"

Duncan did not look up, pawing at the ground with the battered tip of the shovel.

"You've got a rock, Adam." Duncan swept his hand around in an arc, pointing to yellow spray-paint markings. "I'd say a big one, too."

"Never knew it was there."

"It happens," Duncan said calmly. "Anyway, sometimes you have to start digging to find out what's underneath."

"Well, you can take it out, right?" Adam kicked at the loose soil with his good foot and measured the yellow markings in his mind. "It's taking up a quarter of the sunroom area."

"Not that easy. It's pretty big. Might even be a rock shelf..."

"Well," said Adam. "Can we blast it out?"

Duncan smiled politely and leaned against his shovel. "Done a lot of blasting in your lifetime?"

"Well...no," Adam demurred, "but you can pretty much blast through anything. They are blasting in this area all the time."

"Adam, see those windows?" Duncan pointed toward the expanse of glass that clad the back of the house facing the patio.

Adam sized up the circled ring of paint on the ground. "Well, one way or another, it has to go. Otherwise it's going to screw up the plans." Even with his injured ankle, Adam walked away with a determined stride. Not a problem, Adam thought. He's the pro. He'll figure it out.

Adam shuffled past the stacks of lumber and bags of concrete, scaled the shallow swale near the back of the property, and turned down the path that led to the foothills.

Being at the rock was both an escape and a reward; it took him away from the noise, but it also served as his way of restoring his self-reliance. *I wouldn't do anybody any good hanging around the house all afternoon. Mo wants me to relax anyway,* Adam reasoned, *so I'm following orders. And, rather than answering everyone's questions about how I'm doing, I can find out for myself.*

Adam's first two or three moves against the scalloped wall of the boulder proved his ankle could resume its duties even faster than the doctor thought it would. It was a lower, safer route across the face, but still, it was slower going than he imagined. It didn't help that his head was buzzing with other conversations: Mort and the deal, Duncan and the rock, Jason . . .

His occasional grunting and breathing mixed with the coarse scraping sound as his boots fought against the rock face. He felt more than ever that he had to figure out every move; nothing seemed natural. *Guess I'm just a little rusty or wary,* he thought.

Then the quivering started, first in his arms, then in his legs, and finally in his lower back. He arched his fingers to get a better grip on the rock and pivoted his boots to gain whatever traction he could below.

"Lean into the rock, Adam." He was startled to hear any voice at all, but he had no reason to turn around once he heard it.

No way, Adam thought, as he fought to stay suspended in midair by his arms and legs, clawing with everything he had to stay where he was. *If he could only get to the next set of handholds and footholds . . .*

"I'm serious. Lean into the rock," A.J. said again, this time with more playfulness. "Don't fight it; use it to your advantage." Adam's muscles were wound tight by now, so he reluctantly eased his body toward the surface, closing the distance faster than he imagined. He felt the coolness of the stone through his shirt.

"Now just relax," A.J.'s voice took on a calming tone.

Adam's mind was still racing about what to do next, but at the same time, he felt an uncanny safety having his body pressed against the stone. Maybe it was the slight friction, or maybe it was because he was no longer canti-levered out in space, held only by fingers and toes. He felt lighter.

"Now just clear everything from your mind."

"I swear you're a shrink..." Adam's hoarse laugh ricocheted off the stony surface. The issues and concerns in his head were like an overloaded to-do list. The more he tried to do what A.J. said, the longer and more high-lighted the list became.

"Okay, I give," Adam sighed between breaths. "I don't know how to do that."

"Just stay focused in the moment, what you are doing right now," A.J. called out.

Okay, Adam thought; he shook his head, as if the ges-ture would fling all the clutter in his mind off into the air around him. He felt the gritty surface of the rock through his shirt and wriggled his toes and fingers deeper into the shallow recesses.

"Now how are you feeling?" A.J.'s voice sounded closer.

"Better, actually. Good to go." Adam pushed against the footholds as he slid the open palm of his right hand up until he detected the next shallow recess. Push, slide, grip, settle...push, slide, grip, settle. He felt tired again in seconds, but this time he leaned into the rock without prompting.

Adam made another move sideward, but this time, as his search swept across the stone face seeking a break, there was none. After passing his palm over the surface several times, Adam leaned into the rock for a moment, then he pushed back from the surface in a controlled move. He landed catlike on the rock table below, wincing only slightly as the weight of the drop tested his ankle.

"I see gravity is back on your 'friends' list," A.J. chuckled. "Nice move."

"Thanks." Adam brushed the rock residue from his shirt and sat down on the round boulder near A.J. "Even without my climbing gear, it was refreshing to get back up there, even for a short climb."

They both sat for several minutes, feeling the warmth of the early afternoon sun seep through their clothing, the shadows retreating into the base crevices of the boulders around them. Adam was the first to cut through the quiet.

"I'm exhausted," he admitted, although with a wry smile. "I'm accustomed to a good workout, but I'm even more tired than I thought I would be."

"Fighting can do that to the best of us," A.J. said with a slight smile.

"If you're talking about me fighting the rock up there, well, let's face it—it's the rock or me."

"I didn't see the rock fighting you, Adam," A.J. countered. "I saw you fighting the rock. There is a difference."

Several minutes passed while Adam argued the point in his head.

"When did you feel the most tired up there?" A.J. asked, sensing Adam's mental wrestling match.

Adam closed his eyes and retraced his route on the boulder. "It was when I was struggling in my position, fighting to get a better grip. There was a real burn going on and I was feeling it."

A.J. lifted his cap and swept his fingers through his dark hair, letting the few moments of silence settle in between the two of them.

"I remember when I first started climbing," A.J. said wistfully. "Back then I was free-climbing cliffs, not just boulders. The stupid thing was that, as strong as I was, I wore myself out trying to fight gravity. The more I fought, the less progress I made. The older climbers knew what I was doing, but they just let me go—or maybe they were trying to help me and I wasn't listening."

Adam ran his hands over his arms, massaging the still-sore muscles from the first part of his climb.

"Tell me," A.J. snugged the cap back on his head and pressed his sunglasses more tightly against his face, "what was it like when you leaned into the rock?"

Adam felt his shoulders relax as he recalled the moments when A.J. urged him to press himself against the stone surface. "Honestly, it felt damned uncomfortable at first—it felt like I was giving up," Adam admitted. "But once I was against the rock, it felt like I could relax a bit. Funny, that's what we used to do when I was younger. I guess I forgot how to do that."

A.J. laughed. "I'm afraid we often find it easier to fight an obstacle or pretend that it's not there, rather than accept it for what it is and use it to accomplish something worthwhile. In your case, it was not even people you were up against, it was—what can I say—a rock."

"So, you are saying I should just give in to difficult situations?" Adam said ruefully. "In my world, that would put me at a severe disadvantage."

"Acceptance does not mean quitting, Adam," A.J. turned back to look at the face of the boulder. "You did not give up to the rock. You leaned into it, regained your strength, and were ready to make progress again."

"But, A.J., in the business world, my job is to make things happen and there are people who are out to stop me from doing that."

"How do you know they are fighting *you*?"

"C'mon, A.J.," Adam scoffed. "People are either pulling with you or pushing against you. I've been around long enough to know when someone's working against me."

"Maybe, just maybe, Adam, that someone is trying to help you but you don't know it, or that person *is* working with you but in a way different than what you might imagine."

Adam let a lot of time pass. So much time that he felt his body relax deeply into the rock table, his thoughts relaxing with it.

"You're pretty philosophical for a park ranger from Peru. You know that, don't you?" Adam finally said without looking over.

There was no immediate response, only the distant crunching sound of boots on the gravel. Adam leaned up on his elbow and pushed his sunglasses back in time to see A.J.'s form bouncing over a nearby rock and disappearing along the path below.

Adam did not call out to him, but instead leaned against the rock and nestled his sunglasses back onto his face.

Don't fight. Lean in.

Have to sleep on that one, he said to himself as he pulled the brim of his cap over his face and shifted himself into a more comfortable position on the rock.

This is probably as good a place as any.

⌒

Adam felt refreshed when he awoke, tickled out of his nap by the rivulet of sweat that trickled down the side of his neck. It was dead quiet, the afternoon sun commanding the sky, the air warm and still, the only sound the scrape of Adam's boots as he eased himself upright and hopped down to the path heading toward the house.

⌒

"Hey, guys, how's it going?" Adam elbowed his way through the thin aspens at the back of his lot and surveyed the scene before him. Jason had joined Duncan and Cole as they stood near the marker paint that outlined the margins of the largely hidden rock. "Dunc, that rock still got the better of you?"

"Well, it's your rock," Duncan chuckled as he reached down and tussled the fur on Ollie's head. "You bought it. The three of us and Ollie here are just thinking through some options."

How and when did I buy this rock?

"I don't mean to sound rude, but standing around isn't going to get anything done. Can you work on some other part of this project for now?" Adam swept his hand across the view of the backyard. "We have the pool house and the back corner of the property, all the things you said we would get to later. Seems like maybe this is as good a time as any."

Duncan smiled wryly. "Trust me, activity is not the only sign of progress."

Adam sensed it was not a statement that invited a response, so he stayed quiet, softening his puzzled look. Duncan now turned to face Jason and Cole as well as Adam.

"I've spent way too much of my work life getting called in at the last minute to clean up some problem that could have been avoided if others were clear from the start about what they really wanted, what mattered," Duncan said reflectively. "I don't want to do that any more."

Duncan buried his worn knuckles into the fur on top of Ollie's head. "So, if we want a change in pace, how about we think more about that question."

"What question?"

"*What do you want?* That question," Duncan reminded him, as he again started to walk the circle of paint around the rock. "That's a bigger issue than this rock."

"Now you're frustrating me, you know that, Dunc?" Adam followed after Duncan to try to get in front of him. "I thought I already explained what I wanted, remember? You were the one who didn't accept what I showed you."

Jason eased toward Adam, glancing a bit nervously toward Duncan before speaking.

"Dad, it's not a bad question; it's just a hard question, so the answer may not be *right* there." Jason tapped his temple and started to turn back toward the backyard. "Maybe you could give it another run, and take it a step further. You might be interested in what you come up with." Jason glanced over his shoulder with a careful smile. "And so might others..."

Adam's eyes darted among the three of them, then he threw his hands up in mock exasperation, laughing out loud.

"You guys have got to be kidding me!"

Cole and Jason slipped toward the backyard as Adam approached Duncan.

"Seriously, Dunc, what the heck does all this have to do with getting this rock out of here and finishing the project?"

"What are you so tense about?" Duncan asked. Adam stopped his walk as Duncan blocked his path. "Really, why are you so cranked up about this?"

"Because," Adam stood up straight and locked eyes with Duncan, "sometimes I wonder if you're just using this whole rock situation as a way to delay the project because you are not sure how to get it all done."

Duncan was quiet for a few moments, then he carefully laid the shovel on the ground and took a step toward Adam.

"You know, Adam, if you really want to waste your energy fighting a damned rock, go ahead," Duncan said with a steely tone. "But if I were you, I'd be a little more careful about seeing who is in the way before you throw your words around. Someone might get hurt."

Adam felt his breath catch in his chest as Duncan's eyes flashed a rare glimmer of anger but then softened for a few seconds to a look that was almost a pleading. Then Duncan stepped back, grabbed the shovel, and returned to chopping at the soil around the rock.

Nine

———

It was late morning on Sunday and already Adam felt the edginess knifing into what was left of his weekend. It didn't help that he lumbered into the day exhausted from the day before—not from activity, but strangely, from the lack of it. At least three times he tried to concentrate on the novel he had brought to read, and three times his mind and then his eyes wandered off. Even lying on the couch staring at whatever baseball game was on was not enough to coax him into a nap or stop the buzzing in his head. As much as he tried to push the confrontation with Duncan back into the shadows, the memory prodded him, giving him no rest.

The talk with Maureen earlier this morning didn't help, if it could be called a talk. He had been standing out on the patio, trying to get his bearings, when she came up behind him and tapped her finger on the back of his head.

"Hey, in there. Hello?"

Adam reached back to grab her hand, partly out of affection, but partly out of annoyance.

"Lot going on, Mo," he said. "I'm not sure you want in there right now."

Maureen whirled around Adam to face him, her hands clenched at her sides.

"Yes, I do," she said with a measured determination. "That's the problem. You're just pushing on everything and everybody right now, and some of us are feeling a little pushed out."

"I'm not trying to. I have a lot of balls in the air right now and I don't want any of them landing on you."

Maureen sighed quietly, taking a deep breath before speaking. "How are your talks going with Jason, now that he has come all the way out here?"

"Oh, you know," he said. "Fine."

Maureen stiffened. "Adam, he's trying to get his balance, find a path for himself. You're not making it any easier for him."

"I told you our talks have been fine...what else do you want me to say?"

"Fine is not fine and you know it!" Maureen brushed her hair away from her face as her eyes pleaded with him. "I talked with him a lot on the way home from the airport. He needs to know you're okay with where he is right now."

"Yeah, well, I'm a lot more worried about where you and I are on this," Adam said. "I'm trying to get him grounded and moving in some direction and I feel like you compensate by coddling him. Every time I try to help him in my own way, you fight me..."

"I am *not* fighting you, Adam!" Maureen's eyes were glistening. "I wish you would stop fighting *me*!"

They both knew that silence was the only balm for the moment. After a few minutes, Maureen turned quietly away and headed around the back of the house toward the rose gardens along the driveway. Adam retreated to the kitchen and flipped open his laptop. There were several new e-mails, including one from the investment bankers noting the discussions and action items from the finance committee meeting. One that caught his eye was another request for a further review of the synergies from the two earlier acquisitions, with Darren serving as point person. Nothing formal, the note said, just a stress test of the numbers in case the analysts start boring in on that after the acquisition is announced. Still, Adam was baffled that they kept focusing on something that really did not matter in the big scheme of things; moreover, he was disappointed at being questioned *again*.

The e-mail that jumped out at him was the one from Stan, the board chair. "Adam, please call me Monday morning at eight o'clock my time. We need to talk through some options…"

Mort, Adam muttered to himself. He got to Stan.

There is no more time to consider additional options. The way Adam saw it, the board was dithering at the worst possible time: you consider all kinds of approaches and options up front, but once you have the target locked in, you go after it and don't start screwing around with what-ifs. Leadership was all about pressing ahead. Options at this stage were just a way to lobby people away from the strategy and kill the deal by analyzing everything until you choked the thing.

Adam grabbed a pad of paper and drew several boxes—champions, followers, laggards, foes—each with lines connecting them to different scenarios for how the deal could move forward or how it could be blocked.

Adam was wary of pitting people against each other or of simply counting votes and rolling over opposition. At the same time, the importance of the deal warranted a clear view of what it would take to get it over the goal line. The world is not black and white, Adam often told himself, but the less gray area the better.

Within half an hour, Adam had every board member assigned to a box and had projected the likely conclusion should the vote be held today. The profile was more complicated and opaque than he would have expected at this stage. He counted three board members solidly in his camp: Beth, Mike Olson, who was allied with Beth, and Charlie Morris, a respected investment planner who had been elected to the board at the last annual meeting. Three others were pretty cautious and basically were holdovers from Chuck's era. I can't count on them, he calculated; I've never known them to take a firm position on any board measures of this magnitude. That left Stan and Mort. Counting his own vote, Adam only needed one more to get his five votes out of nine, but he was concerned that Stan and Mort were tied in with each other, especially after what he'd observed at the finance committee meeting the week before. If they both voted against the deal, it was done.

The chart at least told him this: he had a lot of work to do.

Adam took Stan seriously—he was board chairman, after all. With his shock of full gray hair, his chiseled face, and his erect posture, Stan commanded a room when he entered. He was always impeccably dressed, and a suit that would drape over those mountainous shoulders was not one that came right off the rack at the men's clothing store. He was neither indulgent nor pretentious in dress or manner, yet underneath his polished exterior was a stocky bearing that spoke to a workmanlike family legacy. Stan was the quintessential gentleman who, in Adam's assessment, used power judiciously. For an industrialist making his fortune in hardscrabble Chicago, Stan knew how to hold his ground and get his way, but he picked his fights and he was never foolish enough to throw a punch he didn't think would land. You would not call him introverted, but he was calm, respectful, and reserved when need be. He admired hard work and was known for extolling the virtues of some of his fiercest competitors when those qualities were evident. He saved his fights for the marketplace, and in person, he had a natural humility that allowed his success to be on display without arrogance. Looking at him, you knew he was successful, but it was equally apparent that it was success hard-earned.

Stan had the reputation and the financial heft to use merely a nudge to move things that would require of others a hard shove; he didn't mind push-back if it was well-reasoned and reflected hard-nosed business dealing, but if you tried to jump him, you would find a brick wall under that custom-tailored suit.

"Stan, this is Adam. What's up?" Adam was up early that morning, and made a point of placing the call within the first minute of its appointed time—too early looks anxious, too late appears indifferent. Right on time conveys respect.

"Adam, I thought the meeting last week was really helpful to understand the questions of the auditors and the bankers," he said. "We need to get them a little more comfortable before they will sign off on an offer."

Adam paused, calculating his response.

"Sure, I agree," Adam said with his trademark tone of confidence. "Anything else I need to know?"

"Well, yes, actually."

Adam felt his jaw tighten as he waited for whatever was to come next.

"Adam, I checked in with Mark because he has been talking to some analysts, just part of his normal CFO rounds of contacts, so it does not kick up any rumors. He has been getting some static from them about our earnings outlook and how well the two acquisitions are performing," Stan recounted in his typical measured tone. "They are marking the months off when we said we would recover the start-up and transition expenses we booked last year. They are pretty interested in seeing us get these new businesses settled in so they can get a clear picture of what kind of outlook we have for next year."

"Stan, is there an issue here we need to discuss?" Adam tried to keep his tone cool with the guy who held the keys to the deal, but he was a believer in clarity.

"Adam, that's the whole point," Stan firmed his tone. "We need to start having more discussions than presentations. I know you are selling this hard, but frankly, we can't afford to pursue this at all cost."

Mort got to him.

"Stan, if this deal isn't right, then we stop it," Adam wanted to be conciliatory, but also felt he had to confront the challenge to his integrity. "I just really believe it is the right thing, and when I believe that, I go after it. It's who

I am. If we start wobbling, all kinds of doubts creep in and the door closes."

"Adam," the timbre in Stan's voice revealed a steelier edge to the discussion, "have you ever thought that if this board is wobbling at all it is not because of the deal but the way you are going after it?"

"Stan, I go after opportunities. That's why you brought me on..."

"That's true," Stan was ready with his volley, "but this is not just a shoot-to-kill expedition. Frankly, we've had a few unpleasant surprises with the integration of the two acquisitions you did. We can absorb that, but a mistake on a deal this size could sink us."

Stan paused to make sure Adam was ready for what came next. "Some of us think that you could be so narrowed in on closing this deal that you are not keeping an open mind on it. I'm not closing the door on this current acquisition, but we do have some concerns—so I need you to work with me, not fight me."

Adam's jaw muscles flexed as he weighed how to respond, but decided to wait for what was to come.

"Adam, we've got the webcast the Monday you're back," Stan continued. "I know that you know better than to telegraph anything in that call, but I think we have to strike a more cautious, or at least a prudent, tone. Otherwise, once we announce this thing, it is too easy for them to see it as ambition rather than strategy. I want them to feel we are very careful and measured, and that we waited for the right opportunity."

"This *is* the right opportunity, and this *is* the right time," Adam punched back.

There were a few moments of silence before Stan's voice rumbled back over the phone. "Adam, that's what I'm talking about. You are a high-rolling business development guy, so they might expect you to roll the dice on this, too. We need to be more deliberate and set the right tone for this. I need to feel more confident that you and I are together on that."

High-rolling business development guy? I thought I was the CEO, Adam stewed silently.

"Frankly, Adam, when you get so charged up internally on this, I worry about what it might sound like in the final negotiations or to the analysts." The conversation was weighing toward being a directive, with Stan bearing down now. "We have to *be* more careful, and *sound* more careful."

"Are you asking me if I can do that?" Adam wanted it to sound rhetorical, but he also begged for a direct answer. He was stunned by Stan's response:

"I'm not asking you," Stan said. "I'm telling you."

Ten

———

Adam was so immersed in his own thoughts that he had walked several hundred feet down the path before he realized he was well past his normal stop at the boulder. He kicked some stones down the path ahead of him in annoyance at his absentmindedness, then he spun around to walk back up the path. He only went a few feet before the realization hit him.

What am I doing? This is just not a good day to climb. He scanned the ridgeline and nearby paths for A.J. but the only movements were the frantic dances of squirrels and lizards over the stony soil.

Adam sank onto the surface of another table rock and wrapped his hands behind his neck, kneading the tight muscles as his mind raced. Being alone with your thoughts is torture, he berated himself, when the thoughts just keeping coming back to the same thing no matter how much you work them over. He loved this job, he wanted to do the right thing, he had a passion for the business and its people—but right now, he was just wrung out.

It was at least an hour before the chorus of sounds around him changed. He did not have to look up when he heard the shuffle of boots on the path.

"Why the look? Care to talk?" A.J. flicked a broken tree branch against the stone, drawing imaginary images on the surface as Adam stared silently into the distance.

"Sure, if I thought it would help much, but it is what it is."

A.J. held off for a few moments, then tossed the branch into the nearby brush and turned to Adam.

"*What* is what it is?"

Adam sighed audibly. "I've got a board member backpedaling on a deal. The board chair is on my case now for supposedly having a personal agenda. I'm afraid my CFO may be tipping our hand unintentionally with analysts. My wife is giving me a hard time about working too hard on vacation. And..." Adam turned back to look up the trail to the boulder, "I don't even feel like climbing a damned rock that I used to climb for fun."

"Adam?"

"I know—take a breath." Adam held up his hands in a plea. "That doesn't make any of this go away."

Adam tried to laugh at his own desperate tone, but knew better than to make a joke of A.J.'s sincerity. He kept waiting for A.J. to say something, but the silence remained. Enough time went by for the sun to peer around the other side of a tree across the path before Adam finally picked up a small rock and hurled it over the edge of the cliff, hearing it rattle through the brush below.

"I'm just not myself right now." Adam stared out across the path, afraid that showing his face to A.J. might reveal the turmoil he was feeling. "Before, I felt I was the right person in the right place almost all the time," Adam shrugged. "If you had asked me a month ago what I did well and what I did not do well, I could have answered that, at least the first part!"

"What's different now?"

"Everything's just awkward and painful right now," Adam rarely indulged himself in sounding desperate, but it felt honest in the moment. "Like some kind of out-of-body experience..."

Adam looked over at A.J. with an embarrassed look, then grinned.

"Not that I have any idea of what an out-of-body experience is like, mind you!"

A.J. laughed, but let Adam continue.

"I feel like I have to consciously think through everything I'm doing just to not screw up. It even creeps into other things, like conversations with my son. Jason and I talked a bit when he got here, but it still seems forced and uneasy. I felt like the wrong word said in the wrong way could have tilted the conversation over the edge."

"Did it?"

"No, it was okay. But I'm not happy anymore with just okay." He battled back the emotions roiling up. "I'm looking for something more, but I'm not sure what it is. I don't want to waste time, you know what I mean?"

Adam turned to A.J. with an exasperated look. "So, am I crazy or what?"

Both men were quiet for several minutes, watching the sun simmering down on the horizon, carving shadows on the boulders and cliffs around them.

"This feeling you have right now, the feeling that everything is unnatural and a bit forced?" A.J. began.

"Yeah…"

"It's okay," A.J. elbowed Adam in the leg. "You're becoming more consciously aware of what's going on around you and what's going on within you. We just need to find where they fit together."

"You're playing shrink again, aren't you?" Adam replied nervously, inhaling heavily and blowing his breath out between tight lips.

"I've spent a lot of time on the trail and have observed a lot—don't take it as anything more than that. You're on the right track. Self-reflection is a good thing, Adam, but not everyone has the stomach for it," A.J. assured him.

Adam felt a bit awkward accepting the indirect compliment. "I'm a little surprised or disappointed in myself, if you want to know the truth." Adam scraped another small stone from the ground and tossed it across the path. "I used to feel like I was the one to make things happen. Now I feel like I'm just reacting to everything around me."

A.J.'s silence was not lost on Adam. Funny, he thought, here I am worried about reacting, and A.J. doesn't feel the need to react at all. For the first time that day, Adam embraced the quiet. It was good to not feel like he had to fill a void, or expect someone else to do so. Several minutes passed before A.J. reached down himself to grab a pebble and toss is over the cliff. He gazed out into the canyon as he spoke.

"In Peru, it's a custom among some local villages to send young men off into the mountains by themselves," he said, with a fondness in his voice. "It is—what do you say—a rite of passage into manhood? There is always a point, maybe half way through those thirty days, when some will try to return to the village, saying the journey has become too hard, that they want to come home. They were always sent back! The journey is hard. And it always seems to get worse before it gets better. It was when the journey got hardest that I learned the most about myself."

Adam thought carefully before saying what was now on his mind.

"You were one of those who tried to come home, weren't you?"

A.J. pushed back his cap, slipped the sunglasses from his face, and looked squarely at Adam.

"I was a much younger man back then my friend."

By now the sun was diving behind the ridgeline, the sky deepening to violet, the sparse clouds outlined in streaks of orange and red. Adam stood up and walked next to A.J., joining his gaze toward the distant panorama.

"You like the mountains, don't you, A.J.?" Adam finally cut through the stillness.

"I do. I love these places."

"Is that why you became a ranger?" Adam's question was casual, as if the answer was obvious.

"I came here to escape," A.J. said quietly.

"Man, don't we all!" Adam sighed.

Eleven

Adam did not like to call anyone on his executive team at home in the evening, so he was surprised at how unhesitating he was in hitting the speed dial assigned to his COO. Part of his maneuver was defensive; he wanted to keep Darren in his line of sight right now. But, despite the suspicions that boiled up at times about Darren's links to the board, he also felt oddly safe talking with him, especially with so many agendas playing out within the board itself.

"Sorry to bother you this evening," Adam sat back on the couch and kicked off his Top-Siders. "I just wanted to check in a bit..." Adam let his sentence trail off, hoping Darren would pick up the conversation and perhaps give Adam a clue to his mood.

"That's fine," Darren replied easily. "You still fighting your good fight with the board?"

Adam was taken aback at first by the characterization, but downplayed it in his mind as just a colloquialism for what Darren had to appreciate was a tense situation.

"Well, I'm trying not to make it a fight, but I think we all need to hang tough about what this deal could mean for us." Adam did not feel the need to posture in front of Darren, but he did not want to leave any doubt in Darren's mind that it would take a unified front by the executive team to swing the votes with the board.

"I'm with you on this, Adam, really," Darren replied. "If you want my opinion, though..."

"Sure, of course." Adam was aware that his fatigue was over whelming any sense of curiosity, and weary of fielding so many opinions when it was his reputation on the line.

"It just feels like there is a lot of fight on this one," Darren said in measured tones. "Do you think we might be pushing too hard?"

Adam noted that Darren said *we*, probably not accidentally. Adam figured it was his way of showing he was supportive, but it also telegraphed that Darren was wary of creating an impression that he was lecturing Adam.

"Actually, I'm a little surprised you think this is a hard push," Adam said. "You're the guy who drives a pretty tough deal with suppliers and partners. I never had you pegged as a guy who backed down." Adam truly admired the results that Darren was able to get out of operations, but his comment was also intended to get Darren into a corner by appealing to his tough side in supporting the deal all the way through. Rather than rise to the challenge, Darren laughed, which took Adam by surprise.

"Adam, I pride myself in not having to draw down your time and focus by involving you in things that are in my court, so you see my results, but you don't always see my method."

"I guess I'm not sure what you are saying."

"Everyone thinks I push and grind to get those contracts and terms, but if I did that, we would probably drive our costs up, not down."

"Why do you say that?"

"I don't fight our suppliers, Adam. I work with their interests and align them with ours. If either party thinks they are getting pushed or taken, my instinct is to pull back." Darren seemed to welcome Adam's question and started to really open up in ways he had not often done before. "What I know is that if we push too hard, they start to worry about coming out on the short end and then they look for other ways to make it up. Pushing against each other just turns the whole effort into a huge waste of good energy. Somebody loses, and usually both parties."

Adam cradled the phone against his shoulder and massaged the soreness in his forearms as he sized up what Darren was saying.

"How do you not get taken advantage of in a situation like that?" Adam volleyed. "You can't just lie down or give in."

Darren was relaxed enough now to jump right on Adam's comment.

"That's why I'm the COO and not you, my friend!" Darren said. "I've been doing these contracts my entire career. I don't give in, Adam, but I do know when it is time to just stop and accept what is at play and what the other party needs to accomplish. Then I can work with that to get to an agreement that makes sense for both of us."

Lean into the rock, Adam . . .

"What if their reasons are at odds with ours?" Adam now found himself more intrigued with Darren's method, but he was still cautious.

"Most of the time, when people think they are at cross-purposes, it is simply that they don't know each other well enough," Darren explained. "So they speculate or assume, which almost always goes to the wrong place."

"Darren, there are bad characters out there..."

"Absolutely, Adam. And if that is the case, I don't deal with them, because after talking with them I *know* their purposes violate mine," Darren replied with conviction. "But I will always try first to understand their intentions rather than interpret their actions. When I do that, more often than not, I find they have a good reason for what they do. Even more important, they appreciate that I respect their interests, so it creates a whole new field of play. I'm not after either/or...I want and/both. Make sense? Adam?"

"Oh, sorry," Adam laughed as he realized he had raced down a mental path while Darren was still talking. "Yeah, makes sense. At least in theory..."

"It does take some practice..."

"Hey, I've taken up too much of your evening," Adam sat up straight on the couch, pawing the coffee table for his notebook. "Thanks for the catch-up. I'll see you next week. Call me if anything gets a little hairy back there."

"Always."

⌒

While Adam went to sleep that night feeling reassured by Darren's comments, he woke up the next morning still haunted that Stan was trying to kill the deal. He just doesn't want to come out and say it, Adam thought. His reputation is on the line. There are so many reasons this deal makes sense; so it's got to be that he doesn't have faith that I can pull it off. And all the while, Adam concluded, he has recruited Mort as his messenger.

Took me a while, but I finally get it, Adam assured himself as he punched numbers into the phone.

"Hey, Mort…Adam." Adam walked around the kitchen and the den as he talked. He knew that it made him sound a little pumped on the calls, but there was something about walking around that kept the blood flowing to his brain, kept him on his toes.

"I was thinking about our talk the other day…" Adam waited to hear an acknowledgement from Mort, but none came, so he continued. "I know I get a little aggressive in situations like this, but I don't want anyone to interpret that as deal heat."

"Is that what you think is happening?" Mort was pretty calm, Adam thought. He was ready for this call, I'll bet.

"Well, sure," Adam brightened at the prospect that Mort wanted to hear his side of it. "It's just my style. You know that…"

"Yes, I have come to learn that."

"Okay, good to have that out of the way," Adam raced ahead, relieved. "I really want to get us all back on board on this. Time is the enemy of most deals."

Mort measured his words. "Yes, time can really be a problem on a deal like this, that part is true."

"So," Adam was feeling more confident, and chided himself a bit for having had suspicions about Mort, "I think we ought to bring this to a vote and get a definitive offer on the table."

Adam heard nothing coming from the phone.

"Mort, are you still there?"

"Very much so, Adam," Mort sounded weary, "but I'm not sure you are prepared for that kind of showdown."

Adam tried to stay calm. "No, Mort, the last thing I want is a fight. I just believe that a vote would clear away the clutter and get everyone focused. If I can arrange that, can I count on your support?"

"I agree it has to come to a vote, but in all seriousness, Adam, are you prepared to lose?"

"Mort, I worry that some people might want this deal to die a slow death," Adam firmed up his tone, feeling that Mort was falling back on him. "Either the board trusts me or not."

"Adam, it's not that simple . . . and that's not giving the board much of a choice."

Adam felt the chill up his back. What was that supposed to mean?

"Mort, we need to move ahead," Adam said briskly. "I want to call a special meeting of the board next week when I am back and get a straight up-or-down vote on this. It's time to make a decision and move on."

"Well, that's really Stan's call, Adam, but you certainly have the right to ask," Mort said. "I just hope you will think about what I have been saying here."

Adam was polite in his goodbye, and hoped he did not sound too hasty in clicking off the call. On impulse, he spun through his speed dial list and punched the screen when it scrolled to the name he was searching for.

"Beth? Adam . . ." he forced a confident tone into his voice that was hardly felt in his gut. "Got a minute?"

Adam had been out on the porch for at least ten minutes and still his breathing was heavy, his pulse pounding. Damn! I never saw that one coming.

The first part of the conversation with Beth had gone fine; in fact, it had reflected the synergy he has always felt with Beth in the board meetings—their dealings had been direct, practical, honest. Adam had asked her if she knew where the rest of the board stood on the deal. No, not really, she had said. There had not been a full discussion yet to air out the views. The only way to know that for sure was to vote on a resolution. Okay, Adam had continued, could she work on his behalf and bend some ears or maybe twist some arms on this before a vote—after all, everyone knew she was all business, and that's all this was about. We don't want this voted down, Adam told her, it will never come back up after that kind of failure.

That's when Beth lashed into him with a ferociousness that had Adam gripping the phone like a cold wrench. What are you asking me to do? Carry your water for you? You think that's what I invested all my effort to do, call in some chits? The words came in blasts, she was barely keeping her fury in check. It was the last thing he expected from her, and the call was punctuated by such an abrupt end that she might as well have hung up on him.

What, he interrogated himself, just happened? What changed? He felt like he was in a dark closet full of cobwebs.

Adam was still lost in thought when Duncan came around the side of the house, carrying a stack of window casings. Adam started to force a hello, but held back, unsure of whether last Friday's confrontation with Duncan was still too fresh.

"Hey," Duncan nodded.

Adam looked down for a moment, then stepped toward Duncan with his hand outstretched.

"I didn't mean that the other day," he said firmly. "Really. Lately, it seems like there isn't a fight I'm not ready to pick."

"I'm okay," Duncan said with a wry smile. "I didn't treat it as anything between you and me."

Adam looked away, mostly from embarrassment, but also to run a mental inventory of his tangles over the last few days. When he looked back at Duncan, it was hard to cloak the bewilderment he felt.

"Ease up," Duncan said. "People aren't fighting you as much as you think. They probably have better things to do. So do you."

Part IV

———

ABUNDANCE

———

Twelve

At first, Adam's conversation with Duncan had seemed to come to an awkward end—it was just another in all the conversations that were tumbling around in his head. But somehow, this last one with Duncan seemed to stick. Maybe I do need to ease up, Adam thought.

From his perch at the kitchen snack bar, Adam caught himself glancing up from his laptop screen to stare numbly out the kitchen window to the spot where Duncan was working. Adam could tell the pace of work was slowing—the demolition work was done, a drainage pipe had been dug into the backyard, and the new overhang at the back of the house was nearly finished.

He's probably waiting for me, Adam realized suddenly.

He grabbed a notebook and pencil from the counter and bounded off the stool and out the back door.

"Hey, Dunc!" Adam waved the notebook in the air and headed for the patio table. "I think I might be able to answer your question."

Duncan walked over to the table and sat down silently as Adam hurriedly scratched out some shapes on the notepad.

"I think I want the sunroom to extend close to the pool so it looks like one whole region of the backyard." Adam was pleased that he was finally getting some creative ideas on paper. "Then I want to wrap the patio all around the pool and have another section of it lead to the backyard where Maureen has her rock garden. I need the pool house to have a side area where we can have a Ping-Pong table. Then I want low-profile solar lights lining the patio as well as the walkway from around the side of the house."

"Okay," Duncan said, jotting notes on the tablet. "That helps me. But keep going. That's still telling me what you want me to do, the work you want done. What I'm asking is, what do you want?"

"What do I *want*?" Adam weighed the words again in his mind, looking over his shoulder and again scanning the backyard. "Okay..." Adam pushed back from the table and faced the backyard, sweeping his arms in a wide arc, repeating the question now as a declaration. "What do I *want*? I want people to come here to relax, enjoy the outdoors, have a good time. I want to make them feel like they are getting away for a while," he said with surprising conviction. "I want the board to come here each fall and enjoy themselves, I want a place for relatives and friends who visit Colorado to feel at home, and I want a place where I can invite some neighbors over to have a good time. I want others to come and relax and have fun."

Duncan had reached for the notepad and pencil, but kept the pencil poised motionless over the page. "That's very good, Adam," he said. "Way better. Now we need to go one more step."

Adam was perplexed. "What's the matter with that? What's the matter with making a place that other people can enjoy? I don't get it."

"You can't *make* people have a good time," Duncan said steadily. "You can't try to make them happy, relaxed, feel at home, or anything. Well, you can try, but you'll just frustrate yourself—and them."

The look on Adam's face telegraphed his complete bafflement.

"Look at it this way, Adam," said Duncan. "Does Mo cook?"

"She's great. She's a natural!"

"What about you?"

"I'm a great eater," Adam grimaced. "Mo doesn't even want me on her side of the counter!"

"Okay, so if you have guests over and Mo is cooking up a storm, are people having a good time being in the kitchen? Sure, because she's having a great time and is relaxed and happy. She knows what *she* wants—to just enjoy being a cook, being herself. Your guests pick that up and it allows them to, well, be relaxed and happy and feel at home. But if you're cooking that day, what?"

"Well, if Mo's not there, we're already in trouble! I suppose I'm running around trying to get everything right, making sure everyone has their drinks, trying to get the food out on the counter at the right time...seeing to it that everyone's happy."

"Right," Duncan laughed. "And everyone is miserable, including you."

"I never thought about it that way," Adam reflected. "So, maybe all that's true, but what I am supposed to do?

I was raised to take care of others before tending to my own needs."

Duncan leaned back on the picnic table. "That's admirable, Adam, but in reality you have to take care of yourself if you ever expect to take care of others. People want to know you, and you want to get to know them. That can't happen when you're too wrapped up in making sure that others get what you think they need."

Duncan crossed his left leg over his right and started rhythmically nodding the toe of his boot as he continued with a lesson that sounded to Adam like it came from somewhere deep.

"Nothing's authentic when you try too hard," Duncan said, his eyes closed, "and others see right through it. If, on the other hand, you can accept the idea of being yourself and doing what gives you great delight, you will have a more positive impact on the people around you. They'll pick up on your energy. And you won't turn yourself inside out trying to live up to your own, and everyone else's, expectations."

Duncan's question was now ringing louder than ever in Adam's mind, but it had a new clarity. So what do I *really* want? Sure, family, this house, the chance to live in Chicago, the CEO job, a successful life. The more he rolled through the list, the more he began to wonder if Duncan was on to something. Those were things he felt others wanted for him, expected of him—certainly they were things his dad, his teachers and coaches in school, his earlier bosses wanted of him. But what did he want for himself?

Adam stood wordlessly for a few moments, then headed deeper into the backyard, first walking pensively around the perimeter of the marked-off underground rock. Then he walked directly back, crossing over the area of the buried rock, not even noticing it this time, nor feeling frustration over the effect the rock was having on the plans. He headed for the rear of the property, turned, folded his arms across his chest, and looked back at the house, something he had not recalled doing since they bought the place. The minutes slipped by as he stood alone, the events of the week slowly fading, replaced by a quietness that he had not felt since the vacation started.

Do you always play hurt? How is it working for you now? What do you want?

Taking a deep breath, Adam strode back to where Duncan was working near the patio.

"Okay, I think I can answer the question now, Dunc." Adam leaned against the patio picnic table and looked back toward the yard. "I want a backyard that reminds me of when I was a boy playing outside all the time. I want a backyard where I can just dig it that I have a place in Colorado, way up here in the clean air and quiet. I want a place where I don't have to play CEO all the time and can hang out, play chase-the-stick with Ollie, read a book just because it is something other than a business book, and walk around in my sandals or even bare feet because it feels so damned good to do."

Adam took another deep breath.

"I know that must sound a little weird coming from me, but that's what I really want."

Duncan's grin split his face. "Okay, Adam, we can do that."

They shook hands silently. As Adam headed toward the house, he heard Duncan call out from behind him:

"Adam, one more thing…"

"What?"

"My name's Duncan."

Adam smiled to himself and reached for the door handle. He called back over his shoulder:

"Hey, Duncan…"

"What?"

Adam started through the doorway and laughed.

"Stop feeding licorice to Ollie."

Thirteen

Adam got up early Wednesday morning and was out on the porch in time to see the sunlight boil up from the hills to the east and hear the birds chattering their wake-up calls in the trees near the back of the property. Duncan and Cole had scraped off enough topsoil to expose a table-sized expanse of the buried rock; to Adam, it made the subterranean behemoth feel even larger.

Adam propped up the back of the chaise lounge and unfurled the magazine he had brought with him. He barely realized he was staring numbly at the pages, his mind adrift with his own mental journaling of the last few days.

Adam was startled by the *click* of the French doors opening behind him. He saw Jason walk quietly past him and stand inside the yellow circle marking the margins of the underground stone.

"Morning," Adam sat up in his chair.

"Oh, hi," Jason turned halfway to look back at his father. "I thought you were engrossed in reading."

"I wish."

Jason scuffed his shoes against the rock, digging at it with his toe. He spoke without looking back at Adam. "How are you feeling?

"Fine. Good." Adam said. "Why? You thinking of heading back to school?"

Jason turned back toward the sunroom. "On Friday. Classes start up again next week. Why? Are you ready for me to go back?"

"I'm sure you have things to do." Adam eased back in the chair and grabbed for the magazine. "I understand that. It's been good to have you here, but you don't have to stick around for my sake."

Quickly turning away, Adam listlessly flipped through several pages of the magazine, but the words were a blur. Tears began to pool in the corners of his eyes. Adam reached up and pretended to brush an itch on the side of his face with his sleeve, but it was no use. A hot tear streamed down his face, and Adam turned even more sharply to the side to shield Jason's view.

What's this all about? I don't even remember the last time I cried. Not sure I've had a good reason, or maybe I've lost sight of the reasons. Get a grip, Adam.

He reset his sunglasses on his face and sank deeper into the lounge chair as Jason wandered over to the far side of the buried rock. Adam did not keep track of how long the silence lasted, but it was broken by the *creak* of a truck tailgate and the *thump* of boots on the walkway from the driveway.

"Hey, Duncan," Adam brushed away the lingering traces of his tears and pushed back his glasses. "Good to see you. Today we move a mountain, right?"

Adam attempted some humor, but inwardly he was feeling anxious about the obstacle the rock posed to the vision he had in his mind for the backyard.

"Actually, Jason and I talked it through last night." Duncan glanced over at Jason. "He has a pretty good idea of what to do with the rock."

"Duncan, I assumed you would know what to do. It's your area of expertise, right?"

"Well, I like to gather as many ideas as I can..."

"He's attending photography school, Duncan," Adam said, keeping his voice low so Jason could not hear. "I'm not clear on how that helps here."

"Well, it may not be his profession, Adam, but he has a good eye for things."

Adam looked over at Jason, who was pacing off the dimensions of the rock, looking down to count his steps—or simply avoiding looking over to the debate between Adam and Duncan.

"So, what's his idea?"

"How about you ask him?" Duncan said. "He's your son. You are the one he is trying to help." Duncan slapped Adam on the shoulder and then walked back down the path toward his truck.

"Hey, Jason," Adam tried his best to sound relaxed, but he could feel the tension in his throat, almost strangling his words, "Duncan tells me you have an idea on how to move the rock."

Jason stayed on the rock, facing away from Adam.

"I do have an idea, but I never said anything about moving the rock," Jason called back.

"Well, we're sure not moving the sunroom." Adam

responded, trying to find a more relaxed cadence in his voice. "What's the idea?"

Adam stared at Jason for almost a minute, waiting for a reply as Jason sat down cross-legged on the exposed area of the rock, idly tracing his fingers on the smooth surface.

"It's a little hard to explain when you are way over there," Jason finally said.

He's right, Adam thought. Adam lifted himself out of the lounge chair and ambled over to the edge of the scarred soil around the rock. He looked down at Jason nervously.

"Duncan told me what *you* really want," Jason said cautiously. Adam felt vulnerable, for some reason, hearing it come from Jason, but he let him continue. "I think that's pretty cool," Jason looked up at him. "I didn't know that about you."

Adam shrugged his shoulders, still ill at ease with the conversation and fighting back the emotions that were bubbling up again. "Yeah, well, you told me to try to answer the question, so I guess I finally did." Adam walked back to one of the yellow lines. "So, what's the plan you have in mind?"

Jason remained stationed on the rock, but leaned toward Adam.

"You told Duncan that you wanted to—what were your words?—just *dig* the fact that you were here in Colorado in the open air, right?"

"Something like that, yes."

"Okay," Jason scampered to his feet, now more animated than Adam had seen him in a long time. "This rock is not going anywhere—but it doesn't have to!"

"What are you talking about?"

"Hang for a second, Dad. Just accept the fact that the rock is here to stay. What if, instead, we excavate the floor of the sunroom, essentially creating a sunken conversation area? We leave the rock right where it is and build the rest of the sunroom around it."

Adam couldn't conceal the puzzled look on his face.

"No, really, Dad, this could be so cool." Jason was leaping around the edges of the exposed rock, stretching out his arms as if the walls and glass of the sunroom were appearing before him. "We could make all this glass and then make the sunken area the same kind of rock as this stone, maybe even have some water feature in it. So get this—people could sit out here anytime, even when it's raining outside, and feel like they are sitting out in the open air!"

"You mean leave the rock there..." Adam was intrigued, but his mind was racing with questions. "How would you balance chairs on the rock?"

"Dad, when you go out to your climbing rock, do you take a chair with you? No, you just sit on the rock. That's all part of the deal. I bet if you have people over, they would think it was pretty cool that they could sit out here on this big rock in your sunroom. It's almost like they are kids again..."

"But what if they aren't dressed for that?"

"You told Duncan that you wanted a place where you did not have to be CEO all the time, and you would just be able to hang out," Jason smiled. "Don't you think other people might feel the same way, that you are almost giving them permission to feel the same way if they see you doing it? Let some other CEO have a stuffed-shirt dinner party. When people come here, they know they can kick back, like it's their own party up on the mountain, just hanging out with friends."

Adam sat down on the rock, as if to test the concept. He pulled his legs up toward him and locked his hands together across his knees.

"You really think this could work?"

"We would have to change some dimensions so the scale is right." Jason formed a rectangle with his two hands, emulating a photo frame, and aimed it around in a circle. "You want the rock to be a feature and not dominate, and we do need room for people to walk around comfortably," he smiled, "or, okay, sit down in a chair if that's what they want. But this could work, this could be really cool."

Jason sat down on the rock, just a few feet from Adam, and returned to tracing his fingers on the rock surface as he waited to hear Adam's reaction.

"The rock would get their clothes dirty..." Adam said cautiously.

"We could sandblast it and polish it. It's inside anyway by then, so it would not keep getting dirty..."

"How would we do the barbecue? This is a closed space."

"Easy, just build a stone chimney that matches the rock."

"Tough to heat in the winter..."

"Not as bad as you think. There would be so much radiant heat coming in from all the glass, you could probably do with just a space heater to get it to a comfortable temperature."

"What if some people don't like it?"

"Tough, Dad. You can't make everybody happy." Jason threw up his hands. "But do you really think people

are going to come over here and see something that different and cool and walk away complaining? You don't
need to try to make those people happy—because you
never will."

"Cost?"

"Already talked with Duncan. Just have to pay a little
more for the dig-out. Still way cheaper than moving the
sunroom over or trying to dig out the rock…"

"Your Mom?"

"Covered," Jason smiled slyly. "She loves it. She
could have plants and grow her herbs out here almost all
year long. But she wants to see what you think about the
whole idea first."

Adam and Jason sat silently on the rock for a couple of
minutes, each testing in his mind where the conversation
could or should go next, each waiting for the other. Adam
took the lead this time.

"They teach you all this stuff at your photography
school?"

"Not directly, no," Jason swelled with confidence. "I
guess I've always been this way, trying to see things differently, imagining space, proportion, scale. I think photography is just a way to put all that into practice."

"And make a living…" Adam kicked himself for
going there, and braced himself for the return fire. Surprisingly, this time it did not come.

"Hope to, Dad. I know I have to—pretty soon—but
I need to give this a shot to see if I can." Jason fell silent
for a few seconds. "I know you were trying to help, Dad.
I needed some space and a chance to check out what I
wanted to do. I don't just want a job; I need to be doing
something I feel I can be good at, something I really enjoy

doing. If I can get those two things right, I think the paycheck will come in time. If it doesn't work, I know when to cut and run and get a day job. I just don't want to quit on this too early.

"And," he said, almost in a whisper, "I need to know you're not giving up on me. You good with that?"

Adam looked over at Jason, who had an odd combination of determination and anxiety painted on his face.

"Yeah," Adam stood up from the rock and looked down at Jason, "I am." He turned back to face the worksite and slapped his hands together. "Let's do it. I'll talk to Duncan."

"Dad?" Jason said more than asked. "Let me do it. Please?"

Adam stepped back toward the patio and flopped into the lounge chair.

"Okay." He said, as he fanned out the newspaper on his lap with a smile on his face. "I'm good with that."

Fourteen

"I saw you and Jason talking," Mo said, nuzzling her shoulder into Adam's side as they sat on the couch. "How did that go?"

"It ended up okay."

"Okay?" Maureen was careful in her reply this time; *okay* was one of those words, like *fine,* that could mean almost anything.

Adam smiled slightly. "No, better than okay, actually."

"Difference being...?"

Good question. Adam had not felt the need to pick the conversation apart; it had seemed so natural. Still, he knew the answer.

"Me," Adam replied playfully.

Maureen's tension eased, and she used two fingers to press Adam's lips into the shape of a smile.

"I'm proud of you," she said, "and you should be proud of you, too."

Adam drew her hand away from his mouth.

"I just wish it had never gotten to this point..."

Maureen gently rapped her knuckles against his forehead. "Don't overanalyze it; just accept it. I think the two of you are getting back on track."

Adam turned his head to look directly at her.

"But what about us?" he asked, cautiously. "I still feel like you and I are on two different sides with Jason. You've been protecting him and all I have been trying to do is help him."

Maureen sensed Adam's tension rising, so she dropped her tone, reached over, and squeezed his face between her hands.

"We're not on different sides, Adam. We both want what's best for him."

They rested together for a few moments, their breathing falling into a natural rhythm.

"You're always trying to help people," she said. "That's what I love about you. But maybe what Jason needs is some space to struggle a bit rather than *either* of us stepping in to make it better."

Adam pressed his elbow into her side.

"You're good for me, Mo."

She leaned into him.

"You're good for me, too."

Adam finished his coffee and resisted the impulse to get up and pour another or put the cup in the dishwasher. Instead, he just stayed on the couch, with Maureen resting against him.

"How's your secret deal going?" she winked at him and smiled impishly.

"Have you signed a nondisclosure?" he elbowed her affectionately.

"Yeah, it was called a marriage license, big guy. That's okay, I don't need to know, but I hope it is going well."

"I can't tell." Adam leaned forward, resting his elbows on his knees. "I can understand some caution early on, but it just doesn't seem like we're moving the ball. At times I feel like I'm the one who has to make everything okay. More recently, I've been wondering if I might be the one mucking it all up."

Maureen had long ago developed the discipline to not ask questions about the board when Adam was working some issue. There were times when she felt she might be able to help him see things from a different perspective, but she was also wary of stepping over that line between work and family that she admonished Adam for violating all the time. Anyway, even though most of the executive spouses knew as much about what was going on in the company as the executives, there was a bit of a code among them that said you did not talk about it, for fear you might end up on the wrong side of an issue.

Maureen sipped the last of her coffee and stirred from her place on the couch, planting a kiss on Adam's forehead.

"Sorry the deal is causing you trouble," she said gently. "Do what you need to do. I'll be okay."

"Duncan," Adam stood near the edge of the patio the next morning, watching Duncan run a string between two stakes marking the outside margins of the excavation area for the sunroom. "I have a question for you."

Duncan rolled up the tape measure and walked toward Adam. "Shoot."

Adam laughed as he started to speak, "Why are you here?"

"That sounds like one of my questions," Duncan smiled.

"Yeah, it does," Adam smiled back. "I learned it from you. But seriously . . . why are you here, I mean right now?"

"You mean instead of three weeks from now?"

"Yeah. Was it the money? Was it because of what I was paying you? Did I make you come here when I wanted you here?"

"Nope," Duncan pulled out the tape measure again and resumed his marking of the ground.

"Doesn't the money matter?" Adam followed him over to the site of the rock.

"I have no problem being paid well for good work," Duncan said without looking up. "But that's not what matters the most to me, and," he stood up from his crouch and faced Adam, "it's not what brought me out here on two days' notice."

"What then?"

Duncan let the tape measure snap back into its housing, as if to punctuate his response. "Cole."

"The kid?" Adam was puzzled. "I thought he was just some apprentice or a helper."

Duncan sat down on one of the patio chairs and tossed the tape measure around in his hand as he spoke.

"He's a student at the vocational school where I teach . . ."

"You're a teacher?"

Duncan held up his hand, signaling Adam to listen.

"Yes, I teach some courses. Three nights a week. Cole's in my basic construction class," Duncan explained.

"His dad got pretty messed up in a car accident a few months ago. He needed some extra money and some summer internship experience, so this was a chance for him to get in a few weeks of work before he has to be back to class next month. I had another project scheduled, but it was about forty miles north of here; this one is a lot closer and easier for him. I talked with my other client and she was okay with waiting until later this summer on her project.

"So," Duncan stood up and hooked the tape measure back onto his belt loop, "it all worked out pretty well." Duncan knelt down on the ground and started hammering some marker stakes into the ground. Adam waited until the first row of stakes was set before speaking.

"But I'm not paying him..."

"I didn't ask you to."

Duncan grabbed the next fistful of stakes and hammered each one in place, aligning them perfectly with the marker string.

Adam put down the book he was reading on the couch as soon as he heard the sputtering noise pulsing through the wall of the den facing the patio. It came from a small backhoe, but being so close to the house, its sound bellowed through the walls. Stepping carefully outside and standing near the side wall of the house, Adam saw Duncan in the seat tugging on the controls while looking to the side of the shovel. Cole stood in front, prepared to target Duncan's first plunge into the soil. Within minutes, they had clawed through several cubic yards of dirt and loose gravel, dumping each load in a trailer attached to Duncan's truck. The *crunch* of the shovel piercing the stony soil blended in with the deep throb of the diesel engine, making a sound that said this was all business. Amid the din, Adam did not hear the footsteps behind him.

"What do you think?" Jason did not look at Adam but studied the movements of the backhoe as Duncan steered the machine through its steady routine—chop, scrape, lift, dump, and then a spin on its axis to repeat.

"I think it will work," Adam reached out to put his hand on Jason's shoulder. It was a wooden gesture at first, but he found his arm relaxing sooner than he imagined. "I think this could really work."

They stood that way for several minutes, somewhat hypnotized by the repeated motions of the backhoe. Jason stayed standing next to Adam as he spoke above the noise.

"I'm glad you like it," Jason said, somewhat reticently. "I wasn't sure . . ."

"Which part—whether it was a good idea, or whether I would like it?"

For the first time in a long while, Adam saw Jason smile.

"Time was, Dad, when I didn't think there was a difference."

Adam instinctively squeezed Jason's shoulder.

"Tomorrow seems to be coming fast," Jason said quietly. "And Duncan plans to take tomorrow off to catch up on some things anyway, so it's good timing, I guess, to leave then."

"I'm glad you're here, Jason," Adam said. "No problem with me if you want to stay longer."

Jason cuffed Adam's neck with his left hand and turned toward the house.

"I'm proud of you, Jason," Adam said, still staring out toward the backhoe, as the tears again swelled up over his lower eyelids. "I love you."

Adam heard the click of the latch opening the French doors, then Jason's voice:

"I'm good with that, Dad."

Fifteen

A.J. was pulling hard on a large rake to clear some brush beside the path near the boulder when Adam came up silently behind him in the deepening shadows of the afternoon.

"Aren't you glad I'm not a rattlesnake or a mountain lion?" Adam chuckled.

"Rattlesnakes and mountain lions don't wear hiking boots," A.J. laughed as he turned to face Adam. "I assume you're here to climb?"

"Well, to tell you the truth, I was hoping you might be able to climb with me today." Adam glanced up at the boulder. "No deep discussions or lessons, just you and me having some fun reaching the top together. You in?"

"Sounds great," A.J. replied brightly. "I've got some extra time before the weekend crowd arrives and I've had my mind set on climbing today anyway. You feel up to it?"

"Never felt better!" Adam placed his gear on the ground and started to change from his hiking boots to climbing shoes when A.J. leaned over and tapped him on the shoulder.

"Mind if we try a different boulder?" he said, pointing down the stone path. They were quiet for the few hundred yards they walked, Adam relishing the clean air, hearing his boots crunch on the stones. A.J. slowed down at a large boulder just off the main path and tucked behind a scrub of trees, and fanned his hands in the air as if to size it up.

"Okay, Adam, here's the climb. You start where you are comfortable and I'll work another face of it. Our goal—meet at the top."

Adam slipped on his climbing shoes and cinched the laces. Then he stepped back from the boulder to ponder its surface while dusting his hands with chalk. Helmet strapped snugly, he took a deep breath, approached the boulder, and passed his palms lightly over the surface.

"Okay—ready when you are, A.J." Not hearing a response, Adam pounced on the rock, easily landing his hands and feet in secure footholds and hauling himself effortlessly up and along the surface. Soon he could hear A.J. around the other side of the rock, the gentle rattle of his flashlight and radio as they scraped against the stone.

Adam felt some twinges in his ankle, but he easily shifted his weight or just rested against the rock face from time to time to recharge. He felt lighter this time, more agile, certainly more relaxed. Maybe it was the lessons that A.J. had given him, but it seemed more than that. He knew from his days in high school that there is a point— you can feel it more than you can make it happen—where you no longer have to manipulate or think about your moves; they become instinctive, mental memory. This was that day for Adam. Now the rock was serving the role it always had before, a place where he could test himself, stretch, and relish being outside and alive.

"Hey, amigo!" he called out to A.J. "You asleep over there?"

"Ha, not me!"

Adam heard a few muffled grunts and scraping, enough to spur him to keep pushing along to best his companion. He was moving catlike now, gliding easily at an angle, enjoying the experience of new areas of the face and new handholds. Nearing the crown, he danced his hand across the surface above him; he had angled too far to one side and he was facing a difficult crown on the rock, one that jutted out several inches, making it seemingly impossible to haul himself over the edge to the summit.

Two weeks ago, Adam would have pushed it—*had pushed it*—but this time he leaned into the rock and carefully considered his situation. If he traversed the rock back to the right in search of a new route, he would have a long trip with no sure reward of success. Plus, he had already calculated that A.J. was making steady progress in his climb, so time was of the essence. He could either reach up to the overhanging rock, leaving his feet dangling temporarily, and hope he had the strength to pull himself over the awkward edge, or he could ease his way back down. The image and pain of his recent fall swept over him.

"Hey, A.J." he called out. "I'm heading back down. I've hit a dead end. You win."

"What? Why? Where are you?" A.J.'s voice echoed off the nearby boulders.

"I'm near the top, but I'm blocked."

"What are your options?"

"Only two, and neither one is good." Adam yelled into the rock, hearing his voice bounce through the canyon.

"Wait right there for me, Adam. I've got an idea. Just stay put..."

Adam shook off A.J.'s call, determined now to make his way slowly down the face of the boulder. He stopped occasionally to shake off some surfacing shame and guilt that came with his self-proclaimed defeat. Landing neatly with both feet on the stony soil at the base of the boulder, he dusted off his hands and stood gazing over the canyon, waiting for the sight or sound of A.J. coming back down. No reason to mess up his climb just because I failed, he thought.

"Over here, Adam." A.J. was bent down, catching his breath, as he peered up at Adam with a puzzled look. "Why did you quit?"

"I wasn't going to push it." Adam said. "Not today. I'm not showing up in Chicago on Monday with another concussion or sprained ankle."

A.J. folded his arms across his chest and looked carefully at Adam, allowing his disappointment to show. "Adam, I was working my way around your left side and had a better view of where else you could go. And I was close enough to the top where I probably could have reached down for your arm and levered you over that crown..."

"Sorry, A.J., I didn't know that."

"I know, Adam. But why didn't you?" A.J. wriggled his cap back firmly onto his head and wiped his hands of the climbing chalk and stone dust. "And why did you come down without first waiting for me as I had asked you to?"

A.J. settled himself into a sitting position on the rock. Adam paused for a moment before responding. "I knew that you were making good progress and so, along with the risk involved, I didn't think I'd beat you to the top anyway. You appeared to have the clear advantage."

"The clear advantage? Adam, we were in this together. The goal was for both of us to climb to the top together, remember? Because of you, we both lost."

"Hey, that's not fair, A.J. I did what I thought was the right thing to do..."

"...given your perception of the challenge and the two choices you gave yourself, yes," A.J. interrupted. "But you lost sight of our goal, and you didn't consider all of the options. You forced a decision unnecessarily. Forced decisions often create bad results."

Adam mulled over the idea for a few moments before A.J. finally broke the silence. "No big deal. We live to climb another day, my friend."

"I didn't mean to turn this into a competition," Adam said sheepishly, pushing his hands back through his hair. "But you also said that I didn't consider all the options up there. How am I supposed to see what I don't see? What if those other options don't always come easy to me..."

"Well, my friend, that's what other people are for. The objective of group climbs is to get *everyone* to arrive at the top safely. What I learned long ago was that the best solution rarely comes from the one who is stuck in the moment."

Several moments of silence passed before Adam looked over to see A.J. leaning forward to unlace his climbing shoes.

"I guess I'm not very good at asking for help, am I?"

A.J. chuckled, then held his hands to the side of his face as if to warm a memory inside.

"When I first took groups on the Inca Trail, they assumed I knew everything," A.J. lifted his sunglasses, showing a disarming twinkle in his eyes. "Ah, if they'd only known! I knew what I had to know, but that was about it. So I would ask those in the group about choices we could make along the way. It helped me to form a trusting relationship with them, and they often saw options I hadn't seen before. Over time, I found myself telling other guides about great new trail finds."

Adam studied A.J.'s dark face for a few moments, trying to imagine him as that much younger man, brimming with energy and ambition, and yet with the foresight to ask questions as often as he answered them. Funny, he thought, it is one thing to be smart, it is another thing entirely to be wise. Adam's pondering was interrupted by a slap on his knee.

"Time to go, my friend," A.J. said, standing upright and looking at the now-inky sky. "Mountain lions come out at night."

Adam stretched out on the couch, tossing his Top-Siders on the floor so he did not get a playful scowl from Mo for putting his shoes on the couch, and rested his feet on a pillow. He grabbed the notebook and twirled the phone in his hand, finally scrolling down to the number he had called just a few days ago. He settled his head into the pillowed armrest as he heard the first ring.

"Hi, Mort. Adam." Adam felt his breath coming more easily this time. "Sorry to call you out of the blue, but I think you were trying to tell me some things the other day, and I was pretty locked in on what I thought had to happen."

Adam reached for the pen on the table. "I've got a blank sheet of paper in front of me. I'm finally ready to listen..."

Part V

UNSTUCK

Sixteen

Adam rolled over and squinted at the clock on the bedside table.

Nine-thirty? How did *that* happen?

Well, staying up until one o'clock will do that, he told himself. It had been Jason's idea to dredge the old camping chairs from the garage loft and set them up on the exposed rock of the patio after dinner. Maureen seemed unfazed about having to step over the stacks of lumber and open trenches to settle in. The stories spilled out—the time the raccoon sneaked into their tent during their first camping trip, Maureen seeing Adam's legs dangling from the broken hole in the ceiling, the hamster that got loose and took up residence in Mo's winter boots, even Jason's revelation that it had been he and his buddies who had put soapsuds in the town fountain that Fourth of July.

Adam brushed aside the covers and pawed the floor with his bare feet to find his slippers. Mo's side of the bed was already partly tucked back in and her purse was gone from the dressing table. Adam shuffled out to the kitchen, surprised by how tired he felt, how leaden his legs felt even after a good night's sleep.

He saw the card with the smiley face propped up on his coffee cup: *Heading to the airport. We tried to say goodbye but you were dead to the world. That's what you get for laughing so hard last night. Oatmeal on the stove. Love you. M & J.*

Adam warmed up the oatmeal in the microwave, poured some coffee, and went out to the porch. The pit for the sunroom was now carved into the dirt and footings for the sidewalls still glistened from the water seeping up into the dry air. A gentle breeze tossed some plastic sheeting attached to one of the poles, the only sound except for some mourning doves cooing from the grove of aspen trees at the yard's edge.

Adam didn't notice him sitting in the high-back chair until he approached the patio table. His legs were crossed at the ankle, with the side of one of his stained and scuffed boots tapping out a steady beat against the side of the other.

"Hey, Duncan," Adam sat down, balancing his coffee cup on the table and perching the bowl of oatmeal in his lap.

"Morning," came the familiar baritone.

Adam settled into the lounge chair to Duncan's left, facing out toward the yard. Duncan was a clean worker. All of the debris, concrete bags, even loose gravel and dirt were cleaned off the worksite. To the far left, there was a fresh stack of cedar timbers neatly arranged by length and thickness, as if they were giant Lincoln Logs, some with notches already cut into the ends.

"Is that it?" Adam pointed with his coffee cup. "Is that the roof for the sunroom? Where are all the bolts, braces, and nails?"

"Don't need 'em."

"Really?"

There was a short pause before Duncan's voice again rumbled from the chair. "You ever study the masters?"

"I went to business school, Duncan, not architectural school," he laughed.

"Masters are masters in any field, Adam. Your house was inspired by a master."

Adam turned around to look back at his house with a new curiosity. "Who?"

"Frank Lloyd Wright..."

"Really? I just thought it was a nice mountain chalet."

"Chalets are taller," Duncan corrected him helpfully. "Frank Lloyd Wright kept his designs low to the ground, played up horizontal lines. He called it organic design. Except what a lot of people don't realize is that he was a minimalist—he used the least amount of material to accomplish his design and structural goals. There is an elegance in simplicity."

"Where did you learn all this stuff?"

"When you like what you do, you try to get better, and that means studying those who do it best," Duncan said, glancing back at Adam to gauge his reaction. "Frank Lloyd Wright believed in having each element work in harmony with another, each drawing strength from the other. It's the combination of geometries that gives the structure its shape but also its endurance. Nothing stands alone."

"So, no bolts or nails?" Adam now looked back at the stack of slotted timbers.

"Don't need them in post and beam construction," Duncan slipped two fingers inside a fold he formed with his other hand. "Each piece has a role—one carries load, another deals with sideward motion, another takes care of expansion or compression. Each can play its simple role as long as every other piece is doing its job."

"They need to rely on one another, sort of..."

Duncan spun around in the chair to smirk impishly at Adam. "You've been out in the sun too long this week, buddy. It's wood, okay?"

Adam laughed at his own attempt at metaphor, then settled back in the chair.

"Is that why you keep things simple?" he finally asked. "I mean you, personally. I never see you flopping around much. You get right to the work at hand."

"Thanks," Duncan said, almost shyly. "Yeah, I like simplicity. You manage complexity by mastering simplicity."

"You know something, Duncan?" he chuckled. "I'm starting to believe your story about being a teacher."

Duncan settled back into the chair.

"Thank you."

It took a while, but Adam realized that Duncan was tapping his foot to the rhythm of the mourning doves' calls. Every once in a while, Duncan would syncopate the beat, creating this oddly comical subconscious duet between the thump of his boot sole and the birds in the distance.

"Sometimes I think you are Grizzly Adams, retired as a contractor," Adam laughed quietly. "There is no other explanation."

"That's what my wife used to call me, Grizzly Adams," Duncan said, without missing a beat.

Used to? Adam felt a slight chill, wondering if he had somehow stepped over a line he never saw.

"It's okay," Duncan said gently. "We were married for twenty years. Good times, most of those years. Even had a kid."

Adam felt Duncan was ready for the next question, but he still worried he was intruding.

"Okay if I ask what happened?"

Duncan never looked back, but the tapping of his toe slowed and stopped.

"I screwed up," Duncan said. "I was head of a construction company and every day there was always something that needed attention. The phone in the kitchen rang off the wall, even in the evenings. My wife would wince, and out the door I would go."

"That went on for years," Duncan explained. "I figured I was doing the right thing by taking care of everything, seeing to it that my family didn't have to worry about making ends meet—although there were times when we created a lot of distance between those ends," he laughed. "I lost perspective. I just assumed it was my job to carry the world on my shoulders."

"When I had the heart attack, she just blew up," Duncan said matter-of-factly, with some of the emotion clearly now at bay. "She demanded that I quit; I said I couldn't, that I didn't know what else to do."

"So, she quit on you?"

"Yeah, eventually—I came home one day to the note on the kitchen table and half the house cleaned out."

The tapping resumed, although this time it was slower.

The wooden legs of the chair groaned slightly as Duncan settled back hard into the seat and reversed the cross of his legs.

"That's the point I was trying to make the other day."

Adam was quiet for a few minutes, feeling selfish about turning the intimacy of the conversation to what was on his mind, but the question was burning him up.

"Are you saying I need to quit my job as CEO?"

Duncan twisted his shoulders to look back at Adam.

"No, people don't have to downsize their lives to have a decent life," he said firmly. "You just have to get real and be okay with who you are, not trying to be something you're not. I would prefer to see people figure that out from where they are rather than have to fall off a cliff like I did."

Duncan resumed his foot tapping, faster than before, with the only other sound being the scraping of the spoon against the bowl as Adam finished off the oatmeal.

"I love my job. I love what I do," Adam said pensively. "I actually think I'm a damned good CEO and I have worked hard to earn that position. Still, there are times when I just wish everything and everybody would back off and stop depending on me so much. Maybe even let me screw up without it crashing everyone else's world, you know?"

Duncan waited a moment before responding, and he managed his tone carefully.

"You really think you matter that much?"

The silence lingered as Adam came to grips with the question. Finally, he smiled and laughed, seeming to surprise Duncan.

"I had been on my first job for about two years when a recruiter called me," Adam said. "I said something about how they were really going to miss me at the company if I took this new job since I was the leading sales guy. You know what he said?"

"I can only imagine," Duncan laughed. "What?"

"He said, 'Stick your head in a bucket of water and then pull it out, and see how long the hole lasts!'"

"Funny..."

"Yeah," Adam said, "odd that I just recalled that conversation."

They both sat back in the lounge chairs for a while, maybe even half an hour, until the sun started to lace through the branches of the aspens in the backyard, washing the patio in radiant heat. Adam didn't know where the thought came from—it was just a hunch—but it erupted into his mind, and he felt he had to ask.

"Duncan?" he spoke carefully. "You built this house, didn't you..."

Duncan did not reply at first, then gathered himself and replied in a voice that sounded more melancholy than Adam expected.

"Yeah, six years ago. Almost finished it, too."

"The heart attack?"

"That, and the divorce." Duncan turned halfway around to face Adam. "I thought I was building it for my family, our future, but then everything went south. I just finished the house part and sold the place to some guy..." Duncan swept his hand toward the eaves over the porch, "...who stuck this porch on it."

Adam was quiet, mostly because he felt humbled, awed by the revelation.

"That's also why you wanted to do this patio job, wasn't it?"

"We all have our reasons for doing what we do..."

In the silence, Adam spent several minutes replaying the view of the home's interior in his mind, pausing mentally more than he ever had at the intersection of beams and pillars in the rooms. Before this, it had all seemed structural, physical. Now, he felt somehow that he was being entrusted with something more than wood and glass.

Adam hauled himself out of the chair, grabbed the oatmeal bowl and his empty coffee cup from the patio table, and was turning toward the house when he spotted the edge of the notepad on Duncan's side of the table. The first three pages were curled at the edges and rumpled, the first sheet covered in swift, sweeping pencil lines and scribbled text.

"Hey," Adam pulled the notebook toward himself, "what's this? We got a plan going here, Duncan?"

"Actually," Duncan said, resuming the tapping of his boot, "we do."

Adam sat back down, intrigued by the sketches. It was the backyard all right, from a bird's eye view—the sunroom with the glass ceiling and the exposed rock as the central feature, with a stone pit to one side that was obviously a stone fireplace and grill. All around the sunroom were walkways of slab stone, each connected by a series of terraced ledges, each with an area for plants and flowers. The far corner of the backyard—the cove area surrounded by the aspen trees and leading to Adam's path to the rock—was left blank, an open grassy area. Finally, a cabana wrapped around the back of a pool, and an extension to one side that had "pool table" scribbled on it.

As much as the precision of the drawings, it was the artistic flair of the sketches that captivated Adam's eyes. The lines were flowing, as if brushed on the page rather than drawn. Each of the sheets showed the backyard from different angles, with perfect, parallax lines, giving each scene an uncanny sense of depth. Even the shadows of the overhead beams and trees were lightly toned in with the side of the pencil.

"I didn't know you were such an artist, Duncan," Adam said, placing the notebook back on the table with a gesture of respect, if not awe.

"I'm not, my friend," Duncan said, as he spun off the chair, hiked up his jeans by the belt loops, and turned toward the backyard. "Must be somebody else."

"I saw Duncan driving back down the road this morning on my way home," Maureen called out to Adam in the den as she plopped her purse and keys on the kitchen counter. "Was he out here? I thought he said he was not working today."

"He just stopped by," Adam nearly lurched from the couch, stabbed the off button on the TV remote, and came into the kitchen, giving Maureen a lingering hug.

"Wow, what's up with you today, Superman?" she purred back, teasing her fingernails down his back. "Somebody must be feeling better!"

"Yes, I am," Adam pressed her face between his hands and kissed her on the tip of her nose. "I can even help around the house today, if you like…"

"I'll take that offer," Mo kissed him back. "And anything else you have to offer…" She laughed coyly as she slid the car keys into the drawer and headed for the coffee carafe on the counter.

"Just one thing…" Adam said sheepishly.

"Ah, I knew there was a catch!"

"I was hoping I could climb the rock for a while this afternoon," Adam admitted. "Just spend some time outside burning off some energy."

Mo grabbed a kitchen towel and twirled it expertly into a rope. "Fine, then," she said as she snapped it at his legs. "Just save some of that energy for me later."

Seventeen

Adam expected to see some other people out in the park on a Friday as the weekend approached, so he almost did not recognize the figure of the person standing in the path leading to his boulder. He was dressed in loose khaki shorts, a black T-shirt, climbing shoes, and a bright blue climbing helmet, with silky black hair curling out the back.

As he came closer, the man turned to face him.

"A good day for climbing?"

They both scampered up the slight slope of the rock table to the base of the boulder. Adam reached out and clasped A.J.'s upper arm.

"No new lessons today, okay?" Adam asked. "I just want to climb."

"Ah, yes! So, that is the goal, right?" A.J. said as he adjusted the strap on his helmet.

Adam stood back for a moment and scanned the surface of the rock, making mental note of the sheared area. He then slipped on his gear and applied a thin layer of chalk to his fingertips. He went first, easily finding his traction points on the rock and feeling refreshed by the warmth of the afternoon sun seeping through his shirt.

"How's the ankle?" he heard A.J. call out from beneath him.

"What? There's an issue with my ankle?" Adam laughed. "I don't know what you're talking about." He could hear A.J.'s climbing shoes scraping against the rough surface of the boulder. Every once in a while, Adam could see A.J. moving up on his left, but Adam took some pride—if not assurance—in staying ahead of him.

Adam doesn't remember much of what they said—most of it was the normal chatter of two climbers calling out encouragement or good-natured ribbing—but he does remember how it felt. It was like he was back in college, just hanging out with his buddies, letting time pass them by.

Adam was getting tired earlier than he imagined, but he was still far from feeling strained. He was continuing to boulder to the crest when A.J. called over to him.

"What's the hurry?"

Adam took in some deep breaths and pressed himself against the rock to slow the pace and ease the pressure on his legs. When he had gathered his energy, he again pushed upward. Within a couple of minutes, Adam reached the crest. He was tired, and his legs and forearms were quivering a bit from the climb, but he felt more alive than he had in weeks. He leaned over the edge to see the top of A.J.'s helmet.

"C'mon, *El Lento*—slowpoke!"

Within another minute, A.J. was sitting at the crown with Adam, unstrapping his helmet and brushing his sleek black hair back, turning his deeply tanned face toward the late morning sun.

"That was fun," he grinned, taking in a few deep breaths himself before stretching back to lie down on the smooth, flat surface. To Adam, it was a natural sauna, and he felt the heat of the sun pressing into his tired arms and legs, melting away the fatigue and, with it, much of the anxiety of the week. He lost track of—or lost interest in—how much time passed.

"I wish my dad was here right now." Adam was surprised how the statement just bubbled up from somewhere deep, but he felt oddly comfortable as soon as he said it. "I always thought he relied too much on the people who owned that shop where he worked all those years. He trusted them for his livelihood. When they finally closed the shop, he was stuck—had nowhere to go. He was forced to start over, and it was very hard on our entire family."

Adam looked over at A.J. to see if he was reacting in any way. All he could see was the sunlight glinting off the surface of A.J.'s sunglasses, his face turned up toward the blue sky.

"I promised myself that would never happen to me," Adam continued. "He pushed me a lot, so maybe he knew how dependent on others he had become and how stuck he had gotten. He didn't want me to go through the same thing. Looking back, he was probably right, but maybe I've taken the lesson too far..."

After a few moments, a slight smile creased A.J.'s face and he spoke without looking over.

"You know what to do, don't you?"

"Yeah," Adam smiled broadly. "Yeah, actually, I do."

Several minutes passed as Adam let the week fade from his mind.

"You said you come here to escape, right?" Adam said without looking over at A.J. "What do you escape from? I mean, this is your day job anyway."

When A.J. did not comment, Adam felt an awkwardness that made him ask again.

"Escape from what?"

"The Shining Path."

Adam paused. "You are sounding like a shrink again. Wait—you mean back in Peru, don't you? I think I once read something about that, but I don't remember much about it."

A.J. pulled the climbing helmet over his face to block the sun's rays from his eyes. The helmet muffled his voice, but Adam could hear a different timbre in his tone.

"*Partido comunista del Perú,*" A.J. said. "The Communist Party of Peru back in the eighties. Cultural revolutionists, they called themselves. In reality, they were nothing more than thugs."

Adam dared not speak, sensing this was the first time in a while that A.J. had spoken about this.

"They were brutal," A.J. continued. "They raided our farms, killed our livestock, jailed and tortured our local police. The government finally caught their ringleader in the early nineties and stunted their growth, but by then it was too late..."

"Too late for what?" Adam leaned up on one elbow. "For whom? You?"

"For my family, yes." A.J.'s jaw tensed. "We lost everything. My father was never found. I left home and took a job as a tour guide on the Inca Trail after that—fifteen years. I never forgot, and I remained bitter."

"Why did you come here?"

"I felt trapped, like a prisoner in my own country. I wanted to see what it was like to be free," A.J. said almost sternly. "I only knew what it was like not to be free."

"Now you know." Adam knew he sounded smug, but it was also pride speaking.

"Yes, I have learned much here and I am blessed," A.J. said. "But ultimately, freedom is only found here." He tightly thumped his fist against his chest.

Adam was rarely comfortable with silence, but this time he was soothed by it, rolling A.J.'s statement around in his mind as he felt the sun's rays coat his arms and legs. After a few minutes, he spoke, but almost as if seeking permission to do so.

"Do you think you will ever go back?" Adam asked. "You know, to Peru?"

"Maybe," A.J. said wistfully. "My brother has been calling me the last few months. Some of the old farms have joined together into cooperatives, to see if that will work. He wants me to come back and manage a portion of the property. Says they need leaders more than farm-hands at this point."

"What did you tell him?" Adam suddenly felt anxious, almost dreading the answer.

"Soon, perhaps. I told him I will come—when I am ready." A.J. sat up abruptly, fastening his helmet and pressing his sunglasses deeply onto his face.

"But today, mi amigo, we climb."

Eighteen

Adam had been lying awake in bed for several minutes, watching the morning sun cast a dull sheen across the bedcovers. Mo had awakened slightly with him, but pressed herself against him, her head resting on his shoulder, and fell back asleep. Adam pulled her hair back gently and started tracing his fingertips on her ear. She stirred and smashed his hand against the side of her head to stop him.

"Don't ruin it, fella," she laughed softly into her pillow, then settled back into sleep.

Adam had not felt this quiet, this calm, in a long time. It was not any one thing; it was just that the last two or three days seemed to be in slow motion. More than ever before, he could vividly recall every conversation, every scene.

You can't think and be aware at the same time. Sometimes slower is faster. Crazy, but maybe that's true, Adam thought. He knew he at least felt he had more energy. Before this past week he had been running on adrenaline, drawing on his youthful, boundless reserves to push things through. Now, it seemed like slowing down long enough to become aware was giving him a chance to gather his energy and direct it, rather than slinging it off like static electricity.

He had felt that same positive energy yesterday when he tore up that sheet of paper depicting his allies and foes on the board.

The more we resist, the less we accept. Leaning in is not the same as giving up.

Now, the first page was sparsely filled with a line of text and a list of board members. That's all I need, he had told himself as he slapped the notebook closed.

Mo stirred and tapped her fingertip against his temple.

"What's going on in there, buster?"

Adam laughed. "You may not believe me, but not much!"

"No, I don't believe you," Mo murmured. "But I can be converted."

Adam sat up in the bed and stuffed a couple of pillows behind his back.

"I keep thinking about this past week," Adam said, without his normal bravado. "A.J. has turned out to be a good friend. We actually did some climbing together. Had a great time."

Mo elbowed him. "You holding out on me? Who's A.J.?"

"Oh," Adam squeezed her arm affectionately, "he's a park ranger, kind of. From Peru. He's been showing me a few things. And listening to a lot of everything else."

"Helpful?"

"Yeah, a lot," Adam smiled. "So's Duncan. Way more than a handyman, just like A.J. is way more than a park ranger. I just have to keep working on what they are both telling me."

Adam and Mo were quiet for a few minutes, then Mo sat up.

"Did you like the plans?"

Adam refolded the pillow and sat up straighter.

"I thought they were great, really great," Adam felt his voice rise. "Pretty amazing, really. I would not have thought of all that."

Forcing decisions often leads to bad decisions. Creating an abundance of options is always the better choice.

"I'll tell Jason next time we talk..."

"No," Adam said gently, "I will."

"Are you leaving tonight?"

"Tomorrow!" Adam grabbed the pillow from behind his head, clutched it above Mo's head, and gave her a sinister smile. Mo had already wrenched her pillow from under her head and she met Adam's first swipe with a wide sweep of her own. They both rolled up onto their knees for leverage, reared back to reload, and attacked again.

Ollie perked his ears up outside in the backyard as he heard the screeching amid the *thumps,* but then curled back up on the patio once he heard the familiar laughter through all the noise.

Nineteen

Shirley already had Adam's daily files laid out on her desk when he arrived at eleven o'clock on Monday morning. She smiled, but she was tense. It had not been easy to make some of the calls to board members on short notice, especially when she had to be so vague about the purpose of the meetings.

"Beth can do lunch," she traced her fingers down the paper calendar she printed out each morning, as Adam thumbed through the files. "You have to be back in time, of course, for the webcast at two o'clock. Charlie can meet you after work today. Mike is on vacation but said call him anytime. I have Peter, Warren, and Pat set for phone calls early tomorrow morning, half an hour apart. The new chairman of the downtown development group is scheduled for eleven o'clock—we have had to push this off twice already, so we should keep this meeting." Shirley continued her staccato rhythm, as Adam added up the energy these next two days would required of him. "Lunch tomorrow is open, but I figured you would want some time before the board meeting at one thirty. You said you already talked with Mort...that's everybody, except, of course, Stan." Shirley sounded uncharacteristically nervous when she brought up his name.

"He's in your office now," she said tentatively.

"Okay," Adam warmed up a smile to cover the pensiveness he still felt. "Really, Shirl. It's fine." He took a deeper breath than normal and mouthed a "thanks" to Shirley before turning toward his office door.

Adam strode into his office, where Stan was sifting through some books in the bookcase that lined one wall. He reached out to shake Adam's hand, then turned back to the bookcase.

"I have not been in here since Chuck left," he said, as if he had thought about what words to use. "I see he left some books here for you."

Adam was uncharacteristically quiet, considering he was always quick with a comeback. This time, he felt he would be intruding if he said anything too quickly.

"He liked you, you know that." Stan slid a book back into its slot with a firmness that caused a *knock* to echo through the office.

"Well, I enjoyed working with Chuck, too," Adam leaned back against the corner of his desk, standing a respectful distance away.

"No, I mean, he really respected you," Stan turned to look directly at Adam. "He liked your energy, your passion for the company. Chuck knew it was time for him to leave when he did..." Stan waited to see a reaction from Adam, but when Adam maintained his slight smile Stan continued.

"He said you were ready to be named CEO." Stan stopped talking, leaving Adam to wonder if that was the end, and whether it was now up to him to say something.

Stan eased himself into one of the chairs. "So, you called me here. You must have something you want to discuss with me? About tomorrow's board meeting, I presume?"

"Actually," Adam motioned toward the two high-back chairs that faced each other to the side of the desk, "I came here to listen."

Shirley was typing a report when Stan came out of the office nearly an hour later. She tensed at first, failing to detect any hints from his facial expressions, then he shot her a gentle smile.

"You keep an eye on him, Shirley," he said, winking at her. "I think we just might keep him," he said as he passed her desk.

Adam came out a minute later, slipping on his suit jacket and checking his cell phone.

"Adam, your notebook?" Shirley stood up to grab it from his office.

"Don't need it!" Adam laughed, pointing to his head. "I think I'd rather just keep the next one up here."

Shirley went back in his office to make sure files were tucked away. She started to close the notebook on the desk when she noticed each of the board members' names written down the left side of the paper and one line of text written across the top.

What do you want?

Adam was three minutes late to the bank club dining room, and sure enough, Beth had already taken a seat, fortunately in a quiet corner.

"Beth, I'm very sorry to be late," Adam shook her hand and quickly took his seat. "I had a meeting go a little long and it would have been hard to cut it off. I hope you understand."

Beth looked up and said, "I would have accorded Stan the same respect."

Adam failed completely to disguise his surprised look.

"We do try to stay in touch with each other," she unfolded the napkin and placed it on her lap with a flourish, "especially when there is so much at stake."

Adam sat back in the chair and took a deep breath.

"That's what I came to talk with you about…"

"Really?" she looked around for curious eyes and ears from nearby tables, and lowered her tone even more. "That's not why I came."

Adam busied himself arranging the napkin on his lap and taking a sip of water, seizing a few moments to gather his thoughts.

"You're right," Adam looked up, a bit grimly. "I owe you an apology."

Adam was readying his next words when, to his astonishment, Beth shook her head easily.

"Look, Adam, you don't owe me anything," she said. "Quite the opposite—I'm here to apologize to you."

Adam was already shaking his head in confusion and disagreement when Beth leaned toward him and pressed her hands against the white tablecloth, looking at him intently.

"Adam, I know you had good intentions when you called me." Beth's face was unreadable at first but she could not resist smiling as she continued, "You were a little awkward in your execution, but you meant well."

"Yes, I'm sorry about that..."

"That's fine, if you need to be sorry, but I set you back. I need to fix that," Beth said resolutely.

The waiter had been standing a short distance away, awaiting a lull in the conversation before approaching. Beth waved him toward the table.

"Salmon Caesar, please," she said, without looking at the menu, then she motioned toward Adam. "Two, I believe?"

Adam chuckled quietly and nodded in agreement. As the waiter turned away, Adam stared down at the table, flipping the fork a few times, then glanced up at Beth.

"You know me well."

"I think so, yes." Beth relaxed in her chair.

"I make it hard, don't I?"

"Sometimes, yes," she said, grinning easily. "But we all do that. Don't think you're special!"

Adam absentmindedly retrieved the napkin from his lap and laid it neatly on the table, layering it back into shape and pressing against the folds with his palm.

"Adam, we're fine," Beth said.

"I was out of line."

"So was I," Beth said, almost sadly. "I guess your call just stirred up some old garbage that I thought I had thrown out by now."

As secure as Adam had come to feel in his relationship with Beth over the years, he was intrigued that she trusted him enough to invite a deeper, more revealing discussion. Still, he was hoping she would make the next move. A couple of minutes passed while they both distracted themselves by taking sips of water and glancing causally around the room. Adam almost jumped when Beth finally cut through the quiet.

"How well do you know me, Adam?"

"Pretty well, I think," Adam said carefully, "which is why I'm still puzzled about why we got into it so badly on the phone. I guess you thought I was lobbying you."

"Well, you were, let's be clear on that, okay?" Beth laughed, but then grew quiet as the waiter came back with their salads. After a few minutes, Beth put her fork down and relaxed more deeply into her chair.

"I got tired, Adam," she said, her eyes drifting off to a place only in her mind. "Years ago I bought into the game that the only way for me to be successful in business—particularly as a woman—was to be fast, tough...and distant.

"I got a lot done, and I'm not ashamed of what I accomplished," she said. "But while externally I got lots of credit, I was surprised by how empty I felt inside. Looking back, what was missing for me all those years was the opportunity to just be myself. With the sale, I decided to step back and figure out how I could move forward in a different way, my way."

"But you stayed on with our board..." Adam probed.

Beth laughed out loud. "The secret is, Adam, that I had resigned from the board, just like I stepped away from several other things I was doing." Beth leaned forward, and said, almost in a whisper, "Maybe you shouldn't know this, but Stan and Mort asked me to stay. The nice thing was that it wasn't because of my banking connections—because I had already dropped all of those."

"Why, then?"

Beth's voice was almost wistful as she folded her arms on the table, her eyes sparkling. "Stan and Mort had something to prove, Adam, and they wanted me to be part of that. We decided to show this business community that there is a better way to do things. Don't let Stan's gruffness or Mort's shyness fool you. They have been determined for some time to create a collaborative atmosphere on the board—we listen to each other, we care about each other, we don't play games, and we accept and respect each other for what we bring."

Beth's face brightened, even though her tone was more determined than ever.

"This was my second chance, a chance to be who I am and show I can make a difference. I owe them for that," she said. "We don't want anything—or anybody—to break that up, and we'll fight anyone who tries."

Adam smiled deferentially. "Including fighting me, I found."

"Well, here's your apology," Beth said warmly. "I wasn't mad at you. I was mad at myself, because our phone call took me back to a place I had been trying very hard to leave behind. Change is hard, and sometimes we fall back. So, I'm sorry, Adam, really sorry."

Adam studied her face for a moment, seeing a kindness that had escaped him to this point.

"Thanks," Adam said. "Apology accepted. You're right, I did need that."

Beth pushed back a bit from the table, folded her napkin, and sat up straight, looking directly at Adam.

"You may not know this," she said, "but the vote to replace Chuck was unanimous, not because we were universally disappointed in him but because we took the time as a team to come to a decision we all felt we could support. We did the same when we named you."

Adam felt his face flush.

"I don't want you to make the same mistake I did, Adam," she said firmly. "You're one of the best business people I've seen in years—and a great person. Don't lose sight of how important it is to be both."

Beth stood up, and Adam quickly pushed back his chair to come to her side of the table. He held out his hand to her, and she clasped it in both of hers, squeezing firmly.

"Adam, please," she said, in the gentlest voice that Adam had ever heard from her, "if you face a tough problem, if something isn't working the way you feel it should, even if you're unsure of your next step, let us in. It will mean every bit as much to us as it will for you."

⁓

The rest of the day was a blur, but Adam felt an energy in the office that had been absent for too long. The webcast went well—there were a few questions about lagging earnings, but no alarm bells went off. Adam even got a question about the potential acquisition and he handled it with aplomb, saying that kind of move was within consideration if there was a good market out there, but it would be considered very carefully. The stock was slightly up at the opening of the market and stayed steady as the day progressed.

⁓

Adam had a sandwich in his office, checked his e-mail one more time, and grabbed his jacket.

It was twenty-five minutes after one.

"How do I look?" he grinned broadly at Shirley as he came out of the office.

Shirley shook her head in mock disdain but smiled back at him.

"I think we'll keep you!" she said warmly. "Do well."

Adam strode down the hallway, swinging his note-book freely at his side, hearing the light *clack* of his heels against the polished wood. He turned right toward the foyer at the end of the hall and slowed his pace. He could hear the chatter inside the boardroom—he could pick out Beth, Mike, Stan, even Mort—but the voices mostly blended into a steady hum, occasionally broken by some laughter.

He grasped the door handle and walked into the room.

Epilogue

Leadership seems easy—until it gets hard.

It *is* a struggle. As executive coaches, we see this struggle played out all too often as smart, caring, well-intentioned executives strain furiously to keep up with the world around them. It is a world that insists that leaders—managers, executives, chief officers—possess the ability to stuff a staggering amount of activity into their day, the stamina to push back against a tidal wave of complexity and conflict, and the sheer force of personality or position to get things done and make decisions. Used judiciously, these are all admirable qualities. Applied too often, however, they lead many to an early exit.

The facts speak for themselves. A decade ago, the typical CEO stayed in the role for nine and a half years. Today? Only three and a half years. The peril is not just for executives but also for their organizations—for 86 percent of CEOs today, this is their first time in the corner office. They know they are struggling—when asked in a recent survey to describe their feelings about their job, executives used words like *anxious, overwhelmed, stressed,* and more. While this tension is most acute at the CEO level, it is not hard to imagine how the sentiments pervade the rest of the leadership team, or the ranks of people who aspire to these positions.

These are smart people; they are industrious, agile, and clearly ambitious. Most of them come to us for coaching not as a remedial exercise but because they are voracious learners and explorers; they want to understand what is ahead and adopt the positive mindset and behaviors now that will shape their lives and work for years to come. Still, they admit that something is "off" between their sense of what they thought executive leadership would be and what it is turning out to be. The notion of having time to reflect, to savor the moments of genuine conversation and interaction, or to pause to explore ideas seems quaint and distant.

The struggle—this path to decline—has a pattern:

Going too fast. Ignorance is not a label that sits easily with any of us, but that is in fact what results when we *go too fast*, relying too heavily on what we know rather than slowing down and becoming genuinely curious about what we don't know. Adam first climbed the rock with the assumption that his past knowledge still applied; he was ready to finalize the plans for the patio without first recognizing his real needs; and he took for granted that the board was of the same mind on the acquisition from the start.

Fighting too much. As coaches, we see executives exhaust themselves (and often their organizations) fighting formidable realities or entrenched interests in their business world, as if yielding or not volleying with equal force is a sign of failure. Whether it was straining to climb the rock when he knew his strength was ebbing, imagining he could just blast an underground rock out of his backyard, or trying to marshal enough votes on the board to overcome what he felt was an opposing faction, Adam spent too much time and energy denying current realities.

Forcing too many decisions. Most executives pride themselves on quickly narrowing down choices, as if that discipline alone eliminates distractions and focuses management's attention and energy in the right direction. The tendency to jam decisions is founded on a mindset of *scarcity*—resulting in a fear that we have to grab for every advantage. Options are brushed aside, and the executive finds himself or herself clawing for that edge. Adam faced many decisions that he had reduced to binary status: beat A.J. to the top or retreat to fight another day; exert a heavy hand in his son's choices or risk seeing him fail; demand an immediate vote by the board or watch the opportunity fade away. In each of these situations he wasted energy and goodwill in the effort.

We too easily repeat these behaviors over and over again with greater and greater determination—and unintentionally augur ourselves into the ground. Further effort only digs us deeper and makes escape or reversal that much harder to imagine, never mind achieve.

⁓

Is there a remedy to the downward spiral caused by going too fast, fighting too much, and forcing too many decisions? Yes. Our experience with our clients tells us that there is. The remedy we pose to leaders in this new era is in some ways radical, because it asks executives to do nearly the opposite of what their prior experiences and successes might dictate. Yet, at a deeper level, they also know what they need to do, and why it works.

As painted by A.J., lived out by Duncan, and ultimately applied by Adam, there are three steps that reverse the decline and mark a radical new path toward a more sustainable and effective model of leadership and growth in today's world.

1. More Awareness

Awareness is more than knowing that you have blind spots; it is having the patience, discipline, and plain old inquisitive nature to slow down and open yourself up to what you do not know or have not yet experienced. As Adam learned at the rock, there is a huge difference between thinking and sensing. The former is a matter of processing what you already know—filtering, sorting, weighing. Sensing, on the other hand, is taking in new information, perspectives, and conditions without the inclination to first judge them. Adam learned to slow down, step back, and take a fresh look at his situation from a range of perspectives. This may appear obvious to some leaders, but most will admit they fail to do it well. This first step is perhaps the most crucial one toward personal, professional, and organizational growth because it renews the mind and helps inoculate you from getting stuck when you apply old methods to new challenges. Only when we "see the field" can we move on to the second step: Acceptance.

2. More Acceptance

It is human nature to overlook obstacles that stand in our path (or pretend they don't exist)—or to fight like mad to overwhelm them. We hate to give in, especially when we think we are right. As Adam learned at home, at the rock, and in the office, acceptance is the mature and reasoned embrace of our current realities. The forces we tend to fight may actually help us, or at least be turned, to achieve some greater accomplishment. It is the notion of not lowering ourselves to the fight. When we reach this point of acceptance—leaning in, as Adam did on the rock—we are in a much better position to direct our energy away from wasteful battles and toward the third and final step in the leader's climb: Abundance.

3. More Abundance

By creating an abundance of choices, we open ourselves up to better decisions. We understand this intellectually, but it takes a different kind of leader to keep many paths open prior to reaching that ultimate point of decision. Anyone who has ever had the luxury of sleeping on a decision and having a new option emerge in the morning knows this to be innately correct. A.J. helped Adam discover new choices at the boulders; Duncan masterfully allowed ideas to emerge over time in the backyard project; and, ultimately, Adam recognized that the diverse opinions and participation of his board could lead to better decisions for the company. The evidence was all around Adam that it is possible to embrace this notion of creating an abundance of options to yield better outcomes.

When you consider these three steps—*awareness, acceptance,* and *abundance*—they seem easy, almost self-evident. Yet, time after time we see executives elbow these principles aside in the cauldron of their day, or even think they are abiding by them when they are not. And to many, they are simply methods to be used when convenient rather than core elements of leadership to be applied at what may feel like the most inconvenient of times.

Yes, change is wrenchingly hard. There is absolutely nothing out there in your market or sphere of business influence that will make this change easy. It really must come from within—you must summon an internal, almost visceral, resolve to go against the flow. It has to be fortified with a fierce belief that *slowing down* will help you get there faster, that *leaning in* to the opposition often provides one with more power than fighting it out, and that *creating options* almost invariably leads to better decisions.

This approach is not for everyone. What the story of A.J., Duncan, and Adam calls for is—no doubt—contrarian leadership. You must choose it. It won't be handed to you. But true leadership demands the courage and stamina to go against the flow. If you don't think it can be done, it will not—and the struggle will remain. If you don't feel you can influence the world around you that much, you won't.

But some do. Some must.

Those are the ones who will.